Virtues Abounding

Virtues Abounding

St. Thomas Aquinas on the Cardinal
and Related Virtues for Today

Mark O'Keefe, OSB

CASCADE *Books* · Eugene, Oregon

VIRTUES ABOUNDING
St. Thomas Aquinas on the Cardinal and Related Virtues for Today

Cascade Books
An Imprint of Wipf and Stock Publishers
199 W. 8th Ave., Suite 3
Eugene, OR 97401

www.wipfandstock.com

PAPERBACK ISBN: 978-1-5326-4418-4
HARDCOVER ISBN: 978-1-5326-4419-1
EBOOK ISBN: 978-1-5326-4420-7

Cataloguing-in-Publication data:

Names: O'Keefe, Mark, 1956–, author.
Title: Virtues abounding : St. Thomas Aquinas on the cardinal and related virtues for today / Mark O'Keefe, OSB.
Description: Eugene, OR : Cascade Books, 2019 | Includes bibliographical references and index.
Identifiers: ISBN 978-1-5326-4418-4 (paperback) | ISBN 978-1-5326-4419-1 (hardcover) | ISBN 978-1-5326-4420-7 (ebook)
Subjects: LCSH: Thomas,—Aquinas, Saint,—1225?-1274.—Summa theologica. | Cardinal virtues.
Classification: BV4645 .O45 2019 (print) | BV4645 .O45 (ebook)

Manufactured in the U.S.A.   JANUARY 16, 2019

Contents

Introduction

AT LEAST IN HINDSIGHT, the moral life in society a couple of generations ago seems a lot simpler. In reality, of course, human living is, always and in every age, complex and challenging. But we can look back with a certain nostalgia at a time when living, choosing, and deciding just seemed easier. There were clear rules. More things seemed black and white. Even if people didn't—and never have—lived their moral ideals perfectly, at least most people in society agreed on what constitutes right and wrong, good and bad. It was generally agreed that any decent person could observe an action and say "That action is right (or wrong). Period."

Times have changed. In contemporary society, we have very little agreement on what is morally right or wrong. Many people no longer believe that there can be hard-and-fast rules that apply to virtually everyone in virtually any situation. Life—and choosing and deciding—seems a lot grayer and muddier. It's common for people today to think that what's wrong for me (because I believe it to be wrong) may be right for another person if they sincerely believe that it is. "Who I am to say?" is a common response.

The Catholic Church, of course, continues to believe in moral rules that can be applied generally. There are some things that are black or white, right or wrong. Still, even contemporary Catholic teaching reflects a greater sense that there is more ambiguity than we might once have thought, and there are more areas in which people really do have to decide for themselves about what's right or wrong for them in a particular situation. There is black and white, but there are also areas of gray.

One of the developments that we see in contemporary ethics and specifically in Catholic moral theology is a greater emphasis on virtues—on the fundamental attitudes and dispositions that should mark the life of the truly good person. There are certainly many reasons for this development.

But in a society in which there seems to be so little agreement about rules and actions that can be seen as right or wrong, a turn to virtues makes sense. Even if we can't agree about rules, most of us can surely agree on fundamental attitudes and dispositions that would characterize a morally good person. We can all agree that every person should strive to have enduring characteristics like being honest, just, prudent, courageous when necessary, and balanced. We might disagree about the particular actions that would display these virtues in specific circumstances, but simply to agree on the fundamental virtues is a critical movement toward some common ground about good moral living in a good society.

In fact, the virtues, virtuous living, and even a virtuous society were a major focus of the moral thought of ancient Greek and Roman societies. Today, many contemporary philosophers have returned to this ancient wisdom to address the moral issues of today. The earliest Christian reflection on the moral life, as Christianity spread throughout the Roman empire, began in the cultural world of Greco-Roman moral thought. Christian theologians and teachers inevitably entered into dialogue with the learning and culture around them and used its vocabulary and categories to reflect on what it meant to live a good life precisely as a Christian. We see this already in the writings of Saint Paul in the New Testament. He adopted lists of virtues from the popular philosophical thought of his time to describe the attitudes that Christians, transformed in Christ, should manifest and nurture (see, for example: 2 Cor 6:6–8; Gal 5:22–23; Eph 4:32; Col 3:12–17). Other theologians in the following centuries, especially before the total demise of the Roman empire in the West, continued this focus on the importance of virtues in the Christian life. But no Christian theologian, before or since, has more fruitfully or systematically advanced reflection on the moral life as a life of virtue than Saint Thomas Aquinas in the thirteenth century.

Saint Thomas's moral teaching in his monumental classic, the *Summa Theologiae* (Summary of Theology), focuses most of its vast attention on the life of virtue.[1] Aquinas doesn't neglect questions of right or wrong actions, moral rules, and from where the rules come. In fact, he tells us that the virtues are the essential dispositions or abiding attitudes that move us to act rightly. But the sheer volume of his reflection on the virtues demonstrates that he is more concerned with the abiding tendencies that must mark the truly good human person than he is with either law or particular actions. In contemporary moral terms, we say that he is more concerned with the

---

1. The *Summa Theologiae* is hereafter abbreviated as *ST*.

kinds of people that we are (our moral character, our "being") than with the specific actions that we perform ("doing"). This is not to say, again, that he ignored the importance of rules and the reality of actions that are either right or wrong; but he viewed them largely from this broader perspective.

Aquinas inherited the substance of his discussion about virtue from the Greek classical world (such as the Greek Aristotle and the Roman Cicero) and from the Christian theological tradition (especially Saint Augustine). But Aquinas was an original and systematic thinker. He brought together in an amazing new synthesis the received insights of classic pagan philosophy together with biblical and theological sources. And he did so with practical insight into the human person and ordinary human living, giving us an enduring wisdom that can still offer enlightenment to us today. Sadly, in the period shortly after Saint Thomas, for a variety of complex reasons, theological attention shifted from virtues to laws, from abiding attitudes to particular actions and the rules that govern them. Only in recent decades have we begun truly to recover ancient and late medieval wisdom on virtues as tools for understanding the realities of contemporary moral living.

The structure of the Thomistic teaching on virtues is focused on the theological (faith, hope, and charity) and cardinal virtues (prudence, justice, fortitude, and temperance). The latter—the cardinal virtues—he inherited especially from classical thought. Looking particularly at the moral life, it is these cardinal virtues that guide and really make possible good moral living. It is these virtues that will form the focus of this book. But Aquinas was a theologian and Christian of deep faith and prayer. For him, the truly good human life cannot be fully understood except in light of our salvation in God through Christ. And the moral life, more specifically, cannot be understood apart from the life of faith.

Because of his faith perspective, Aquinas places his discussion of the cardinal virtues after his teaching on the theological virtues. While we can reach an understanding of prudence, justice, fortitude, and temperance in themselves apart from faith (as Aristotle had done), we cannot, in the end, understand their true shape apart from seeing them in relation to faith, hope, and charity. In the same way, every person must strive to grow to be more prudent, just, courageous, and temperate; but he or she will never arrive at the fullest possible human development without growing in these virtues in the context of nurturing the growth of the theological virtues.

This book focuses our attention on the cardinal virtues that guide our moral lives (and thus, on the "moral" virtues) in light of the wisdom of Saint Thomas. We will, however, diverge from him a bit in presentation by holding the discussion of the theological virtues until the final chapter. This will allow us to focus on the cardinal virtues on their own in the hope of arriving at a clearer understanding of them. In fact, we live in a pluralistic society in which an understanding of the natural virtues is what we can reasonably hope to share with those around us. It is important, then, to be able to appreciate these virtues on their own terms (even knowing that, without what faith offers, we do not yet have a complete picture). Having examined the cardinal virtues in themselves, we will then look at them in their true and essential theological context. My hope, then, is to deviate from Aquinas's order of presentation for pedagogical or explanatory reasons without erring from his fundamental teaching about the faith context in which these virtues must ultimately be understood.

In fact, there have been many discussions and explanations of Saint Thomas's teaching on the cardinal virtues (see the bibliography at the end of this book). Some of them have been detailed and scholarly. Others have attempted to paraphrase or summarize his thought for contemporary readers. Still others have taken his thought as a launching point for a broader or more contemporary reflection on virtues. Some have taken on the structure of the cardinal virtues and then left Aquinas's thought behind altogether. All of these approaches can offer valuable and useful contributions to our understanding of virtues and of good moral living. Our purpose is a bit different. What this book attempts to do is to look not only at what Aquinas has to say about the cardinal virtues, but also and especially at what he says about the virtues related to them. We understand the cardinal virtues better by seeing the virtues that Saint Thomas sees as related to them; and we better understand these related virtues by seeing them in the light of the cardinal virtues. And it is this entire picture of cardinal and related virtues in Saint Thomas's thought, I believe, that sheds important light on the challenge and shape of the contemporary moral life.

The word "cardinal" comes from a word that means "hinge." For Aquinas, all of the other many moral virtues can be related to these four cardinal or "hinge" virtues. And his reflections on these other virtues deserve more attention than they have been given. For example, very little has been written for the daily lives of contemporary readers about the way, according to Saint Thomas, religion is a virtue related to justice; the virtues

of magnanimity, perseverance, and patience are related to courage or fortitude; and the way that even our desire to know and our idle curiosity must
be moderated by virtues related to temperance. But these are fascinating
and amazingly enlightening insights for us today. With this in mind, we
will look at the cardinal virtues and, in each case, look at related virtues and
their practical importance to us today.

It must be noted that Aquinas's thought is extraordinary for his
breadth and for its detail and precision. He wrote in a different time—in
a different language but also in a largely different philosophical and theological world. For contemporary readers, his writings can be difficult to
understand, and his tendency to divide, subdivide, and draw multiple lines
of thinking into a comprehensive whole can be maddening (even when he
is most insightful in doing so). In this context, we are not attempting a close
and exhaustive discussion of Saint Thomas's thought on moral virtues. We
will not examine in detail every virtue that Aquinas mentions. Our intention is to draw contemporary insight for the ordinary person who wants
to live a good moral life (or really, more properly said, a good human life).
About that, Saint Thomas Aquinas has many valuable things to say. We will
strive to stay close to his thought and presentation, drawing out its wisdom
for today, without feeling the need to paraphrase, summarize, explain, or
bring into contemporary idiom every aspect of his sometimes dense and
complex but immensely valuable thought.

In light of our purposes, I do not offer either footnotes or citations to
Aquinas's works. These could potentially be endless and distracting for the
average reader. I am following rather closely the order of Saint Thomas's
unfolding, and I begin each chapter which is devoted to a particular cardinal virtue by indicating where it can be found in his *ST*. By looking at the
table of contents of a translation of the *ST* (some principal English transla-
tions and where they can be found on the internet are mentioned in the
bibliography), the reader could easily locate the precise section in which
Aquinas addresses the particular related virtue under discussion. Further,
the bibliography at the end of the book lists works that can offer summa-
ries or paraphrases of Aquinas's writing. (If you are not familiar with the
ST, it will be useful to know that it is a three-volume work. Volume Two,
which focuses on morality and especially on virtues, is broken into two
parts—and so, there are what are rather oddly referred to as a "first part of
the second part" [I-II] and a "second part of the second part" [II-II]. Each
volume or part is broken into "questions" [e.g., II-II, q. 41 means "question

41 in the second of the second part—in this specific example, the question on the virtue of temperance in itself].) Thus, if the reader wanted to follow up a particular point in this text by looking at the *ST* itself, he or she could look at the table of contents in a modern translation of the *ST* to find the pertinent question. The statements of the questions as they appear in editions of the *ST* are generally clear indications of their contents.

I have not set out to prepare a textbook for classes in moral theology. The approach here is not properly scholarly nor academic. (I do sometimes offer the original Latin name of the virtue under discussion when there is not a good, agreed-upon English equivalent.) At the same time, I have taught a graduate-level course on the theological and cardinal virtues several times, and I have wished for a small supplemental text that could offer some discussion of the virtues related to the cardinal virtues. In that sense, this is the book that I would have liked to have had. It is my hope that Christian and especially Catholic faith formation programs and groups will find this text useful for group discussion and sharing. I hope that Christians—and people more broadly who just want to be better—will find this book a help for the journey to a more authentic human way of living their ordinary daily lives.

1

The Virtuous Life

(*ST* I-II, qq. 55–70)

WE ALL ASPIRE TO be morally good and upright people. If we were asked what being "morally good" means, we might respond that it means doing good things and avoiding bad things. It means treating people fairly and decently. As Christians in particular, we might include obeying the commandments—and, even more particularly as Catholics, we might add that being good includes following the church's moral teaching. But if pressed to say more, we might begin to move from what morally good people do or don't do, to the kinds of attitudes that they have: caring, generous, balanced, and honest. And it is precisely in moving in the direction of such attitudes that we move into the realm of virtues.

It is one thing to do good on one occasion or from time to time. It is quite another to do good reliably and consistently. Even wicked people can do good things occasionally. Being truly good—as distinct from being able to do the right thing every once in a while—involves being able to do good in a regular and dependable way. Virtues are precisely the abiding dispositions or tendencies that enable us to be reliable and consistent in right action.

In fact, a virtuous person can be relied on to guide us to the good even when the right response seems difficult to determine. Let's say, for example, that we need some help in deciding on a specific course of action in a complex situation with a number of possible options. We say: "Let's go talk to George. He's always good at working these kinds of things out" (that is, he has the virtue of prudence). Or we might be asking one another, "What's

1

the fair thing to do here? Let's go ask Mary because she is all about fairness and has a good sense for thinking through such things" (that is, Mary has the virtue of justice). "How much should we drink at the party tonight? Let's watch to see what Marty does" (that is, he has the virtue of temperance). These examples suggest that the people mentioned above have an abiding and reliable tendency to act in good ways. It is part of who they are. And their virtue is a reliable tool in the moral life for themselves and for those around them.

What is Virtue (and What is Vice)?

Aquinas defines virtues as "habitual dispositions" that lead us reliably to do the good. A virtue, he says, is a *habitus* which suggests that a virtue is a kind of habit. But it is not the mindless kind of habit that we can fall into—habits like tapping your fingers on a table while you wait, whistling when you walk along, or endlessly clearing your throat. A virtue is certainly not a habit like smoking. For Aquinas, a *habitus* is a kind of alteration in our natural abilities. The virtues that guide our moral lives are a kind of modification in our will—that is, in our ability to choose to act for the good in certain areas of our life. For example, we acquire the virtue of chastity by resisting one temptation after another, by choosing to act in a chaste manner when we could have acted otherwise, and picking ourselves up when we fail and starting again. Gradually, these repeated decisions and actions modify our will itself—our power to decide—so that it becomes easier to be chaste reliably and consistently.

Virtues are similar to the kind of habitual skills that we learn with repetition. The tennis player or golfer practices the right swing, over and over again. At first, she must think through what she is doing: how she is holding the racket or golf club, the position of her feet and her elbows, etc. When she notices a mistake or when someone offers her a helpful observation, she makes adjustments and tries again. But she keeps repeating the action until it becomes second nature, and she can perform her skill well without thinking about it. Eventually, she no longer has to think about her swing at all—except how she can make it better and better. The same could said about habituated skills like typing, playing the piano, dancing, or cooking. The virtues that guide our moral life are like these learned and practiced skills, except that virtues are habits that guide our actions to seek what is truly good.

The Catechism of the Catholic Church speaks of virtues as "firm attitudes, stable dispositions, habitual perfections . . . that govern our actions, order our passions, and guide our conduct according to reason and faith" (CCC 1804; see the *Catechism*, paragraphs 1803–45, for an overview of the virtues). Virtues make us firm and strong in being directed to and in doing the good. In fact, Saint Thomas says that they bring us smoothness, ease (power), and promptitude in accomplishing the good. For example, if I possess the virtue of temperance in eating, when I am faced with a tempting but unhealthy snack, I can resist it without struggle, resolutely, and without vacillation in making the right choice. We all know from experience that it is quite possible to see very clearly what we *ought* to do, but find ourselves too morally weak to do it—or at least the right choice takes a lot of time and internal effort to accomplish. Virtues give us spontaneity and even a kind of joy in doing the good.

One of the principal characteristics of a virtue is that it is always directed to the good. The virtue of fortitude or courage enables us in a reliable way to overcome what stands in the way of attaining a good. The police officer, for example, shows courage in facing danger to protect lives. When, on the other hand, someone is able to face obstacles to accomplish evil, it may look like courage, but it is not. It is a firm resolve and fearlessness in pursuit of selfish or evil gain, but it is not courage. Thieves who are willing to face threat of arrest or the possibility of an armed homeowner in order to steal certainly possess an ability to face danger, but they do not possess the virtue of courage. In the same way, the virtue of prudence enables us to consistently choose well; but it is craftiness or shrewdness, not prudence, to know how to efficiently and effectively do evil.

The virtues aid us in doing good and help us to do so consistently. Once we have them, they endure within us unless we begin to act against them. It is possible, for example, to have the virtue of justice, but lose it by one unfair, unjust action after another. It is not usually just one act of failing to respect what is due to others that undoes the virtue of justice, but many such acts over time. In the end, virtues do not determine our action or prevent us from acting against them. They do, however, make it more unlikely and even difficult to do so.

Habitus is a vice, as well. It is the opposite of a virtue. A vice is a habitual disposition or an abiding tendency to do evil. Like moral virtues, we build them up, one decision at a time. Once we have them, they give us smoothness, ease, and promptitude in doing evil. The vice of dishonesty grows one decision after another, progressing from little white lies to more significant untruths, from occasionally to regularly. Eventually, telling lies can be like second nature. Like virtues, vices do not determine my action—I still have the possibility of choosing rightly—but it will be far more difficult to do so. This explains why we can sincerely repent, for instance, of a vice like backbiting. We go to confession and receive absolution and divine help to do better. But if we truly had a vice, it remains in us. It is true that God is helping us, but at a natural, human level, that modification in my will (the *habitus*) remains there. Sadly, I will struggle to avoid acting on that particular vice until, one temptation resisted after another, I have overcome it.

In his famous *ST*, Aquinas devotes most of the second part (that is, two whole volumes) to the virtues. He tells us there that the virtues and vices are "intrinsic principles of action." When it comes time to decide and act, we carry within us (or sadly we lack) the inner power to decide and act in the area of that particular virtue. In addition to these interior empowerments to act, Aquinas says that there are three extrinsic forces (principles) at work in our deciding and acting: grace (exterior, in the sense that it comes from outside of ourselves—that is, from God), law (of various kinds), and the devil. Ideally, all of these principles of acting (except the vices and the devil, of course) function together in us so that we can be reliably guided and strengthened in doing the good.

Types of Virtue

Aquinas identifies a number of categories of virtues. One of the principal ways of distinguishing these broad types is the way in which the virtues come to us. The kinds of virtues that we have been thinking about so far are acquired by our own effort. Not surprisingly, then, we call them acquired or natural virtues. Among these virtues, there are some that guide and empower our intellects—that is, our understanding, our thinking, our reasoning—and these are called intellectual virtues. The virtues that shape and guide the will in order to choose and do the good are called moral virtues. Aquinas maintains that, although the intellectual virtues are essential, they are not really, strictly speaking, properly virtues in the same way as the moral virtues. This is because, by definition, all virtues are aimed at the good. But one could potentially use one's ability to think or reason for an evil end.

Principal among the moral virtues are the cardinal virtues (prudence, justice, fortitude/courage, and temperance). The word "cardinal" comes from a Greek word meaning "hinge." For Aquinas and for the classical tradition, all of the other virtues are related to these four fundamental moral virtues. They will be the principal focus of the following chapters. In discussing these four, Aquinas does not neglect some of the other major virtues that are related to each cardinal virtue, and his teaching on these virtues is insightful and helpful (and, sadly, often neglected in discussions of the cardinal virtues).

Beyond the virtues that we can acquire on our own (always, of course, with the help of grace) are the virtues that God gives us directly. These are the infused or supernatural virtues, and the principal of these virtues are the theological virtues of faith, hope, and charity. These virtues cannot be acquired or built up on our own. The infused virtues are God's gift to us in order to empower our natural virtues, but more particularly to help us attain more than a merely human fulfillment. God alone can give us faith to know God, hope to expect divine union, and charity to enter into a mutually self-giving friendship with the Trinity. Although they are gifts and come to us with grace, the infused virtues must be embraced and nurtured within us so that they can function more effectively in our daily lives.

Virtues and Becoming Fully Human

Saint Thomas maintains that every human being is naturally inclined to "happiness" (beatitude), but not to happiness understood in a superficial way. Rather, every human person is naturally disposed to find the true happiness that comes with being fully and truly human. Traditionally, this has been referred to as "perfection," not in the sense of flawless and without failing, but in the sense of fully and authentically developed. To say this another way, we all naturally tend to true moral excellence—or really, the excellence of our humanity itself. We inherently tend to a kind of moral beauty which is the person fully and properly developed.

As Christians, we know that such human fulfillment can only be found ultimately in union with God. In Christian faith, we know the shape of such authentic human development through the teaching and example of Jesus who is both the perfect revelation of God and the perfect realization of authentic humanity. Implicitly, all people tend to this "perfection" in God; but even without this as an explicit orientation, every human person is directed to their own authentic development at least at a natural level. While this pursuit can never be complete without its transcendent orientation, it can be real enough at its own level and become the path to a true human goodness. We know, in fact, from experience that many people without Christian faith live higher moral ideals and manifest more virtuous lives than we who profess Christian faith.

We naturally tend to our own "perfection," but we are sinners. We are sometimes blind to good and to the means to attain it. And we are sometimes too weak to choose goodness when we can see it. Our natural desires can pull us in different directions, blinding our ability to know the good to be done as well as our ability to accomplish it. We are sinners, and life and the many choices to be made can be complex and difficult. The virtues (aided by grace) help us to order and empower our ability to know and do the good, thus helping us to choose our own authentic development as persons. The virtues form us so that we can become our best selves as human beings.

In the *ST*, Aquinas first discusses the theological virtues of faith, hope, and charity. This makes perfect sense since it is these virtues that are given to us by God so that our lives, attitudes, and choices can be directed to our truest fulfillment in divine union. A discussion of the natural, acquired virtues follows at length. And while his teaching on these natural virtues can be studied on their own—as we will be doing here—it is clear that he means for them to be understood in the fundamentally theological context which he has already laid out.

The virtues help us both to do good and to become good ourselves. As "intrinsic principles" of human action, the moral virtues direct us to make the right choices and to perform good actions with ease, smoothness, and promptness. At the same time, the virtues together form our overall moral character—the kind of people we are. Acting consistently for the good builds our character as it draws us closer to what it authentically means to be a human person: someone who is able to decide well (prudence), treat others with the respect that is due them (justice), confront obstacles that stand in the way of doing the good (fortitude/courage), and maintain a true passion for goodness balanced with other well-ordered natural human appetites (temperance). The virtues help us to do good and to become good in the consistent doing.

The life of virtue is a way of living that pursues true human excellence, precisely as a human person rather than in a particular skill or external achievement. In this sense, the virtuous person seeks to live a life that is authentically worthy of the human person rather than a life that is controlled by selfish desires and intentions. The virtuous life is the pursuit of a true moral beauty—the human person at his or her human best, and thus as God has willed—and the true living out of our fundamental human dignity. We are most genuinely ourselves when we are people of virtue.

But the virtuous life of individuals exists in a broader, communal, and societal context. It is an essential part of the classical sense of virtue, inherited by Aquinas, that good persons make for good societies. Virtuous persons contribute to communities and to a society of virtue. Or, to say it in the reverse order, in order to have a truly good society of any kind—a society worthy of human persons—its members must be men and women in pursuit of virtue. One does not have to share the profoundly social and relational understanding of the human person held by Saint Thomas and classical authors in order to share their conclusion: we live together in a healthier and more human way if we can each decide well (with reference not only to our own good but to the good of others), if we are disposed always to give to people what it is due to them, if we can overcome what stands in the way of realizing the good for ourselves and others, and if we can bring our natural passions into a right balance with what is good for us and those around us.

The Interrelationship of the Virtues

In reality, we are all a "mixed bag" of virtues in the process of development and of vices that are hopefully in the process of being de-habituated or weakened. We have not yet arrived at a fully developed moral beauty or excellence. Our moral character is not yet as sterling as it could be and ought to be. This, then, is the task of the moral life for us as human persons and as Christians: with the help of grace, to become what we were meant to be. We must be continually at work in order to grow in virtues and overcome our vices.

For Aquinas, all of the virtues are interrelated and mutually dependent. Each of us, in the end, is one unit. In fact, the "unit" doesn't always work together in harmony. Our appetites can pull in different directions. We can know the good to be done with a crystal-clear vision, but find ourselves unable to carry it out. We can seem to possess one virtue in its fullness while seeming deficient or even totally lacking in others. But more deeply and always, each of us is a single unit. Our intellect, our will, and our appetites all come together in a single, unique individual. For Aquinas, because of this fundamental unity of the capacities within ourselves, if we could fully possess one virtue, we would necessarily possess all of them. And, if we truly lacked one, we would lack them all.

Even though this interrelationship of virtues is not always clear as we continue along life's moral path, there is a profound truth here. We might think of a public official caught in some public scandal concerning some personal transgression or interpersonal infidelity. Politicians—like ministers, teachers, and every other human being—are prone to fall. I raise this example only to say something about how our vices and virtues exist in an inseparable way within each of us. Some voters considering this scandal-ridden official's possible re-election might want to separate his or her "private" life and personal virtues and vices from the person's public responsibilities and capabilities. But each of us is a unit, and our virtues and vices are interconnected within us. If I am unfaithful or unjust in my personal life—unable to act in a just and temperate way—how could it be that this failure in virtue would not impact other aspects of my life, private and public? Of course, to some degree, we are all a collection of vices and virtues that can be distinguished but not easily and completely compartmentalized. Even though we might find it practically useful to focus our energy at a particular time on overcoming one vice (for example, gluttony) or growing a particular virtue (for example, temperance in eating), we can never rest content until we have overcome all of the vices and developed all of the virtues. Only then will we have arrived at a truly worthy, excellent, or beautiful human life.

In a particular way, Aquinas notes that there is something of the cardinal ("hinge") virtues in all of the virtues. Every virtue involves the ability to know the proper means to realize the good (prudence). Every virtue requires the ability to keep the good of others in mind (justice). Every virtue depends on the ability to balance and order our desires in order to seek what is truly good (temperance). And no virtue can function unless the person has the ability to confront what stands in the way of the virtuous act (courage/fortitude) and the good to be realized.

With this brief introduction to the virtues in mind, we now turn to each of the cardinal virtues and to its related virtues (and vices). We do so in the order laid out by Saint Thomas in the *ST*.

2

Prudence

(*ST* II-II, qq. 47–56)

DECISIONS, DECISIONS, DECISIONS—LIFE IS full of decisions. Most of these decisions are small and virtually inconsequential: What should I wear to work today? Shall I have water or lemonade with lunch? Shall I go grocery shopping today or tomorrow? Other decisions are quite important for me and for the people who could be impacted by my actions: Should I change jobs? Is it time to retire? Should I tell my friend that I think that she is about to make a big mistake?

These latter decisions can be very important indeed. And, even though it might not be immediately evident, even those smaller decisions may have some more significant import depending on the particular circumstances of the day: Maybe, on most days, it doesn't matter at all what I wear to work. But what if today I have a job appraisal or a special presentation to be made? For most people, the decision between water or lemonade at lunch is just a matter of taste, but what if I am a diabetic or in need of losing weight? The decision to go shopping today or tomorrow can be quite indifferent. On the other hand, the very thought of going out grocery shopping today might be little more than a subtle avoidance of something else that I should be doing or a failure of proper time management that could potentially impact others—those, for example, who either expected me to pick up the ingredients for tonight's dinner or those who had a right to expect that I would have spent the whole day preparing my part of our joint presentation for tomorrow.

None of these decisions exists in a vacuum. I come to them as a person who has a history of making decisions—some well-made, others not so much. I come to each decision as a person who has made many, many decisions in the past. And these decisions don't simply exist outside myself. They don't just result in actions that have reality outside of me as a decision-maker. In fact, in a real way, each external act exists within me before there is any external movement. My actions can have lasting impact on me long after it has passed from my active memory or the recollection of others.

We probably don't often think of it in this way, but the fact is that we make ourselves to be through the choices we make. We aren't formed into adult human beings simply by what happens to us, what we are given, or what is done to us. We are also the agents of our own becoming. If, by choice, I do good deeds—if I perform acts of kindness, generosity, service—I make myself to be a certain kind of person. If, on the other hand, I do the opposite—perform selfish, unkind, or petty deeds—I make myself to be a very different kind of person, perhaps someone who, on reflection, I don't much approve of. Each day, with each choice of consequence, I am making myself to be, for good or ill. I am making myself to be the person who will one day stand before the God who created me and has loved me through it all. And because our decisions are matters of such personal consequence to ourselves, we want to make sure that we make those choices well.

Every decision of consequence impacts me, and many of these decisions also have direct or indirect impact on others. The choices I make can have consequences well beyond my own little personal world. My actions and my chosen omissions effect the people around me, for good and for ill. And so, in deciding, I must not only decide with a narrow, selfish or self-centered reference to myself. I must also be able to decide in a way that will be good for those with whom I am in relationship and even for the broader community. In fact, it is unjust to be concerned only for myself or to act only for my own narrow good. It is unjust and unloving.

Perhaps the interconnectedness of our personal actions is clearer today with our more contemporary globalized consciousness. We know, for example, that our individual choices about the use of energy and water, the disposal of our waste, and the preference for locally grown produce can impact the environment. Our choice of the cheapest possible products purchased from big chain stores can lend support to unjust labor practices in those places where those cheap products are produced. But the basic message of the social import of our individual decisions is not exclusively a discovery of the last decade. The classic 1946 Christmas movie *It's A Wonderful Life,* for example, focuses on a character who is offered a vision of what the life of those around him would have been like without him and his seemingly inconsequential choices. It is the same scheme as Charles Dickens's nineteenth-century classic *A Christmas Carol,* in which Ebenezer Scrooge is taken on a journey through the impact of his choices.

Prudence is the virtue that enables us to maneuver through the countless decisions that constitute our daily lives—decisions that must be made well, not just in reference to our own lives but with reference as well to the lives and well-being of others and of the common good. It is prudence that guides us through the changing and sometimes complex circumstances of each situation and thus of each choice. If we have the virtue of prudence, we will be able to make these choices well, and they can usually be made without inner struggle or plodding reflection, but rather "with ease, smoothness and promptitude." If we have the virtue of prudence, our decisions just seem to come together and "work" for our good and the good of others.

What the Virtue of Prudence Is

The word "prudence" may not have a very positive resonance or connotation to the modern ear. "Being prudent" can seem related to "being prudish"—that is, to being excessively concerned for modesty or propriety—or prudence may be too easily or exclusively associated with being cautious (even over-cautious) suggesting that the prudent person is always one who errs on the side of delay or hesitation in action. Or, finally, we might think of a prudent decision as one in which a person is willing to lay aside principles or values for the sake of strategic and pragmatic gains. ("Well, yes, that is a worthy goal, but we need to be prudent about this.") In fact, the virtue of prudence sometimes urges immediate action rather than delay. And prudence is precisely the virtue that aids us in the assessing, balancing, and prioritizing, both of our values and our principles in light of practical considerations in a particular situation.

For Aquinas, prudence is the abiding inclination to decide well. Like all the virtues, it inclines us to the good with "ease, smoothness, and promptitude"—that is, when we possess it, the right choice comes more easily, with less inner turmoil and struggle, and more quickly. In Aquinas's schema, prudence is, properly speaking, an intellectual virtue. It serves our knowing. But its focus is practical. It is knowledge for the sake of and directed to good action. And so prudence could also be called practical wisdom, or wisdom in practice.

Prudence functions at a number of levels. It is the ability to size up a situation and to discover what's really at stake. It helps to identify the good to be sought in a situation in which there may be many possible goods—not in an abstract or theoretical way, but concretely in these particular circumstances. Prudence doesn't ponder which of several goods like family, success at work, camaraderie, or personal satisfaction are, abstractly considered, the higher value. Rather, it helps to identify which good is more urgent or important in this particular situation in which I am pondering, for example, whether it would be best for me to work late tonight on an important project with my coworkers or to go home to my family to spend some quality time with them. All of the goods mentioned above may be at play in that one decision, and it is prudence that enables us to sort it out— again, not theoretically but practically for this situation at hand.

Prudence ponders the ends to be sought, but it is especially concerned with the means to attain a worthy end. In fact, there can be many ways to get things done, some that would be more efficient, others that would be either more expensive or economical, and still others that might be shady in a moral sense. Prudence helps us to identify and choose the right means to attain the good in concrete situations. And it is in this regard that prudence is concerned with those principles and rules which might guide us to act rightly in the situation which we are currently facing. Prudence helps to determine which rules apply and how they apply (or don't). It is prudence, for example, that recognizes that being in a library requires silence; but, in this situation, people need to be informed of some emergency or that a fellow student won't mind if I quietly ask a brief question about our common research project.

To be morally good persons, we must not only decide rightly; we must also live well. Prudence is the possession of the morally mature. Prudent people are able to see more broadly what goals they should pursue at any given period in their lives. They know how to prioritize the various ends that they hope to attain and how to take the necessary steps to attain those life goals. They also know when a goal has become unattainable or when changing circumstances or new horizons make clear that previous plans are no longer the best. A prudent person is one who knows how to act appropriately in different circumstances with a variety of people. In fact, when guiding principles or rules are unknown or the complexity is great, we can turn reliably to the person of prudence to lead us to the right choice in this situation.

Since the virtue of prudence aims at attaining the good by the right means, it presupposes that the person is seeking the good. Only those who want to do the right thing and who desire to be good can be prudent. As we will see, Aquinas speaks of counterfeit forms of prudence which are really just a kind of shrewdness in getting what we selfishly want. In fact, it is a kind of selfishness that prevents real prudence from doing its work.

Prudence in Relation to Other Virtues

All other virtues must be guided by prudence. While it is, for example, the virtue of temperance that properly orders our desires, resisting the force of unruly or disordered appetites, it is prudence that enables us to determine what must be done or avoided in an actual situation in order to act in a temperate way. Let's say that I am trying to eat more healthily, and thus temperately resist unhealthy foods and portions. It is prudence that tells me I had better fill up on something healthy before going to the birthday gathering, eat the salad and soup deliberately before the main course arrives, or not to go to the grocery store on an empty stomach. In the same way, it is courage that inclines me to leap into a river to save a person who appears to be drowning, while it is prudence that ponders my actual ability to swim, the strength of the water's current, and the reality that I have a family at home that depends on me. All the virtues must be prudent, and only the prudent person can be truly just, courageous, and temperate. All of the moral virtues aim at good actions (whether just, courageous, or temperate), and every good action must be prudent. In sum, then, prudence seeks the good in every action; it makes one's actions good, and makes the person performing that action good.

At the same time, prudence depends on the other virtues. If we do not possess the other virtues, we cannot be fully prudent. If I cannot properly order my desires (temperance), I will not be able to see what is truly good, nor will I be able to choose and perform the right means to attain an authentic good. If I lack sufficient respect for other persons and what is legitimately theirs (justice), I will not be able to size up a situation accurately to see what is at stake and what must be done. And if I am not able to reasonably moderate my fear in the face of perceived danger or threat (courage), I will not be able to accurately assess all of the possible means of attaining a worthy end. Alternatively, excessive fear might exaggerate the actual threat and so cloud my judgment of the worthiness of the good that is at stake in this situation, or the fear might weaken my resolve to actually move forward with what needs to be done.

The Necessary Elements of Prudence

Aquinas identifies eight essential aspects or integral components of prudence. Without these, prudence cannot be complete. In fact, he doesn't offer a lengthy discussion of them, and so it's not surprising that different theologians have interpreted their meaning in slightly different ways. But our purpose here is not the perfect understanding of Aquinas's thought, but rather the broader insights they can offer us. Frankly, the identification of these eight components can seem to bear the scholastic mark of comprehensive dividing and subdividing, but their usefulness nonetheless remains clear to any understanding of what it means to be truly prudent.

In our day, it is all too easy to neglect much serious thought at all about what constitutes good decision-making. We can tend to make decisions based on a "gut reaction," on an intuition, or loosely on "what seems best." We could profitably think of these eight elements as the components of any good decision, though Aquinas is speaking of them as elements of the virtue of prudence itself—as what constitutes our abiding inclination to decide well in every situation. In this sense, they are not so much "steps" in making a decision or a kind of "checklist," as much as they are what must consistently come together within ourselves in order to decide and act well. Further, to think of eight distinct components might tempt us to think of decision-making as a necessarily long and ponderous affair—and there are situations in which it might unavoidably be so because of the serious weight of the decision or its complexity—but recall that a virtue lends "ease, smoothness and promptitude" to action. To develop the virtue of prudence means precisely to have brought these components together in an effective and efficient manner so that decisions can be made without undue delay.

Before we examine these elements individually, it might be helpful to ponder an example of the complexity of coming to a prudent decision. We can then begin to see some of these components in action even before we identify them explicitly. Let's take a case where an important decision must be made about initiating a medical treatment on behalf of an unconscious loved one. The Catholic moral tradition and church teaching offer the distinction between ordinary and extraordinary treatments to help us work through such questions. Basically, this involves a prudent proportioning of the benefits and the burdens that a proposed treatment might offer to a particular patient. We must try to recall if our loved one ever spoke about her wishes if such a medical situation should arise, or at least about the values that she held. Clearly, we must understand the situation itself and its impact on our loved one and those in relation to her. We must ask ourselves if there exist some principles or rules to guide us—at least, for example, the prohibition of anything that would constitute euthanasia. We must seek counsel both to understand the diagnosis and prognosis, as well as about relevant principles and courses of action. Perhaps there are people who have our respect and who could offer perspective and counsel because they have faced similar situations. We must ponder possible options and their likely outcomes in light of the people involved. We must try to foresee, as best we can, what might go wrong. We must proceed with a certain measure of caution to see if our choices can and must adapt to unexpected developments. All of this is based on the necessary presupposition that we truly want to make the best decision possible for our loved one, based on her wishes, unencumbered by any self-interest on our part.

Not all decisions are as critical or as complex as those that can arise about life and death medical treatments. Yet our little example begins to reveal the many elements which make up the virtue of prudence that must guide us through good decision-making, most especially where there are no clear-cut or black-and-white answers. Aquinas tried to make the functioning of prudence clearer by identifying eight such components.

A first component of the virtue of prudence is what Aquinas calls memory or remembering (*memoria*). Good decision-making is not just a matter of knowing and applying principles. It also involves the ability to draw accurately from practical experience and lessons learned in the past. Have I ever been confronted in the past by a situation like the present one? Are other situations similar to this one known to me? What can be learned from them? What normally happens in similar circumstances?

The truth is that sometimes we face decisions about which we lack any experience that could now be helpful. At the same time, there are many people who never seem to reflect on the experiences that they, in fact, have had in similar circumstances. Others never seem able to draw lessons from what they have experienced. Every experience is different, and rarely does history repeat itself in all significant details, but we can draw important knowledge from our previous encounters with similar situations. Perhaps this conflict or argument with this particular person is not the first. What went well or not so well in previous encounters? I have had to confront a coworker or a subordinate at work in the past. What worked well and what didn't? What did I miss the last time that I encountered a problem like this? It would be imprudent to treat similar situations as if they were completely alike; nonetheless, the past can sometimes yield practical wisdom to guide decisions in the present.

It must be said that an accurate remembering of past experience is not as easy as it might first appear. We know that our memories can become very cloudy in a short time. Studies suggest that many of the details that witnesses in court sincerely believe to be correct may not be. Our memories can be shaped or obscured by emotion or unconscious self-interest. We can recall situations in a subtly self-justifying manner. To remember accurately and without self-deception is no small accomplishment, and it requires a person who is balanced, mature, and self-critical.

A second element of prudence is an ability to grasp principles or rules that may apply or guide decision-making in this case (*intellectus*). Are there reliable and relevant principles, and how are they to be applied in this specific situation?

We live, of course, in a culture that often does not accept the idea that there are general principles that can be applied to individual people independent of their personal choice to accept those principles or rules. Subjectivism, in a popular sense, is the belief that each individual person ("subject") is the source of their own right and wrong. And so, in our society, it can seem to make perfect sense to say "I personally don't believe in sex outside of marriage, and so it would be wrong for me. But who I am to say that my judgment applies to others? If they sincerely believe that sex outside of marriage is acceptable for them—and they aren't hurting anyone else—then it would be morally acceptable for them." Traditional Catholic morality and the church's moral teaching, on the other hand, is based on the presupposition of an objective right and wrong, independent of any individual's feelings or opinions about them. And so it is possible to say, "It's not my place to judge you for having sex outside of marriage; but I can say that, whatever you personally think about it, such sex is objectively wrong."

Whether or not we accept such objective moral judgments and the principles and rules that flow from them, virtually everyone would surely agree that there are some fundamental human values on which we can agree (e.g., justice, fairness, honesty), and even common principles that are drawn from practical experience about what works for good and what doesn't. *Intellectus* is that component of prudence that identifies principles and ponders how they might reliably be applied to a current situation.

A third aspect of prudence is a readiness to seek counsel—a desire and an openness to learn from others (*docilitas*). Situations can be very complex. We can easily run across decisions about which we have no knowledge or experience. Other people—perhaps older, wiser, more experienced, or more educated in this matter—might offer valuable insight for what is going on in this situation, what is at stake, and how best to respond. We must be "docile"—receptive and teachable.

The virtue of prudence, then, cannot grow in a person who is close-minded, stubborn, or too proud or too lazy to ask for advice. It also presupposes that we really want to know what is right and how we might come to know it. In traditional moral theology, we speak of vincible and invincible ignorance—that is, a lack of important knowledge in decision-making that could be overcome or not. The point here is that we can be responsible for our failure to gain the knowledge necessary to make a sound decision. This points to the related traditional distinction between culpable and nonculpable ignorance—a lack of important knowledge for which we are blameworthy or not.

Fourthly, prudence requires a kind of shrewdness or acquired skill to size up a situation quickly and arrive at a sense of what a good response would require (*solertia*). A shrewd person is able to pick up on clues and subtleties in a situation—to "sniff out" what is really going on. It is therefore a kind of practiced intuition. This nimbleness of mind is not opposed to, but rather balances, the more reflective identification of principles and the considered acceptance of counsel. It is especially important when unforeseen circumstances arise. Prudence, drawing together all of these elements, ensures that decisions are neither ponderous and sluggish nor overly hasty.

Solertia is particularly important in unexpected or sudden situations that demand an immediate response. Some decisions may be slowly—even leisurely—pondered; others cannot. Fire personnel, law enforcement officers, and soldiers must often make quick decisions in dangerous circumstances, and it is this particular component of prudence that is essential here. But situations requiring *solertia* need not be so dramatic. Parents of young and active children, for example, must also often decide and act quickly.

A fifth component involves the ability to think through and compare alternatives, to make comparisons between possible options and their relative merits (*ratio*). What are our options here? Which of them are likely to be the most effective, the most costly, the quickest to arrive at a solution, the one that will serve the most urgent values in this situation, etc.? The point here is particularly the ability to think or reason through what must be considered for a good decision. We must be able to actually bring together and think through lessons from past experience, counsel offered, available principles, and the rest.

Foresight is a sixth element of prudence (*providentia*). This is the ability to foresee or project likely outcomes and consequences, as well as possible contingencies and variables in any option seriously under consideration. How likely is it that the action under consideration can actually accomplish the goal in the manner that we hope and currently expect? What might arise in trying to carry out each option? How might each option impact other persons directly or indirectly?

A seventh element is a kind of internal review of the distinctive circumstances and possibilities of the current situation in light of the other components (*circumspectio*). It involves bringing together in an overall review what has been under consideration in light of the situation as it is. Different circumstances in different cases—even when there are many similarities—may yet require a different response. Let's say, for example, that I am about to make known some sensitive information to a group. But when I walk into the room, I see a person whom I had not expected. His or her presence may move me to quickly reconsider the urgency of giving the information, the amount I might share, or if it is possible or preferable to delay until another time. Absent that one person, it might have been judged differently.

Finally, prudence requires caution in moving forward. Aquinas is not suggesting undue delay in actions that must be taken, but the fact is that not everything can be foreseen or planned in any decision. Prudence demands that one proceed with continued attention and readiness to adapt as needed and as possible. If I am going to say something true but critical to someone who needs to hear it, I may be cautious about how I choose to say it and continue to attend to the cues I am getting in order to adapt how I am speaking the truth in this situation.

Again, these eight elements are not a checklist for decision-making, but rather integral parts of prudence itself. For our purposes, it is less important to identify and understand each of them than it is to see the kind and breadth of components that make up the virtue of prudence. It is precisely our ability to draw on each of these components in one decision after another, choice after choice, that develops the virtue of prudence and thereby makes the process of decision-making easier and smoother. Later in this chapter, we will look at what constitutes prudence's contrary—the vice of imprudence—but here we can already begin to see where prudence might break down and imprudent decisions can find their source.

As we have said, for Aquinas, strictly speaking, prudence is an intellectual virtue that guides moral actions. It is perhaps no surprise, then, that his account of prudence is very cognitive. The elements that we have examined focus on using the knowledge that we already possess, on acquiring more knowledge, and applying that knowledge to concrete situations. And in our day, in which it seems that many personal decisions are based on simple intuitions and feelings, he may offer a useful counterbalance in that regard. Still, from a more contemporary perspective, we can see that emotions can also play a broader and more positive role. Today, for example, we can speak of an "emotional intelligence" by which we can identify and manage our own emotions, harnessing them to make good decisions and to act firmly when appropriate. In the same way, we are able to identify and empathize with the emotions of others, allowing us to more accurately and fully size up a situation and ponder an appropriate response that is in keeping with the legitimate emotional satisfaction of those involved. This is not contrary to what Aquinas himself has taught, but the possible positive role of emotions may be clearer today than in his time.

Types of Prudence

We might usually and appropriately think of prudence as the virtue that aids us in our personal decision-making, guiding our decisions about our own personal lives. But Aquinas notes that we are all in relationship with others, and some of these relationships demand more specific forms of prudence. This is especially true for those who hold leadership in communities and must make decisions that concern the common good in a more direct way. And so, in addition to personal prudence, which is concerned with decisions about our own lives, he identifies domestic prudence (decisions within the family context), governing prudence (which concerns leadership of political communities), political prudence (which is necessary for citizens) and military prudence (in the conduct of war).

Aquinas does not address these types or species of prudence at any length, but it may be useful to ponder the insight that he is offering us. Certainly, spouses (and especially parents) must make important decisions which impact not only themselves, but others within the family, as well as the health of the family unit itself. Such decisions can be very complex and involve the juggling of multiple responsibilities within and outside the family, attending to all the members of the family as needed, managing with available resources, finding quality time together, etc. Domestic prudence looks to the good of all in the family in the midst of multiple factors and things that are good.

Ruling or Governing Prudence

As we have seen, prudence must also be just. Personal prudence cannot be inattentive to the impact of our decisions on others and even on the community. As inherently social and relational beings, we must all have concern for and contribute to the common good of the communities to which we belong. But attention to the common good—without neglect of individual persons and smaller constitutive groups—is a special concern of leaders and a special focus of the prudence that they need. Aquinas calls this "ruling" or "governing" prudence.

Our personal decisions can be very complex, with many variables to be considered. Add more people to the picture, and it only gets more complex. At the political level, whether it is a small town or a nation, leaders must make decisions that take into account multiple groups and their needs and rights in the midst of a variety of complex economic, cultural, environmental, and even global factors (to name just a few). Decision-making of this type requires a great prudence that can rise above purely personal concerns or the concerns of the leader's own group or interests. All of the elements of the virtue of prudence identified above must come into play in an inner harmony.

But leadership is not just political in the sense of those who govern political communities. Religious communities, parishes, and every other institution have their leaders who must make critical decisions. Thinking of leadership at a scale much smaller than nations or cities, Saint Benedict, in his famous monastic rule, says that an abbot must possess the virtue which he calls "discretion, the mother of virtues" (*Rule of Saint Benedict*, chapter 64). Benedict says that the abbot, as the leader and teacher of the monastic community, must know how to arrange things so that the strong remain challenged while the weak are not pushed beyond their ability. The abbot, he says, must be "discerning and moderate," and he must "show foresight and consideration in his orders." He must know how to prudently rub the rust (faults) off the vessel (the monk) without breaking it. Following his teaching on the qualities that the abbot should possess (*Rule of Saint Benedict* 2), Benedict moves immediately to the importance of seeking the counsel of all, including the youngest. Quoting the Old Testament book of Sirach (32:24), he concludes, "Do everything with counsel and you will not be sorry afterward."

In our day, leadership tends to be more collaborative and shared governance. Aquinas's teaching on prudence is no less valid, though perhaps it must be considered in a broader context. For him, prudence is a virtue, which means it resides in an individual. In that sense, leaders must be prudent in collaboration with other prudent leaders. The structures for communication and shared decision-making must facilitate the influence of prudent decision-making for the good of all.

Political Prudence

Aquinas wrote in a time of monarchies. He considered the prudence of the rulers and the largely docile prudence of their subjects. We, on the other hand, live in a time of democracies and of models of shared governance at the institutional level. Even in contemporary religious communities which may still have a "superior" and in dioceses with their bishops, governance is more collaborative. But, especially in political institutions, this development makes the prudence of citizens even more essential. It is no longer simply a matter of prudent obedience, but rather the prudence of individual citizens in shaping the future of their cities, states, and nations, especially through participation in the political process.

Think especially of the real prudence necessary in responsible voting. Issues in a pluralistic and complex world are very difficult to follow, but many people tend to get their news from television, and they form their political opinions based on slogans and very one-sided blogs. But voting responsibly in a complex world requires all of the factors that Aquinas identifies as the elements of prudence. This includes the willingness to make the effort to be informed, to take counsel beyond my own group, and to consider the real complexity of issues and the values at stake. In a particular way, the prudence of citizens requires a consideration, not only of my good and the good of my group, but of the common good. A political candidate, party, or platform might benefit me and my concerns, but the prudence of a good citizen in a globalized world must consider one's own good and the right political choice in a much, much bigger context.

Military Prudence

One wonders in a world of nuclear arms and terrorism if it is prudent to wage war at all. Time and time again, we have seen that violence begets violence, and the seeds of the next war are planted in the one that just seemed to have ended. Surely it is the prudent thing to seek peaceful resolutions to international problems. Sadly, our political leaders do not always seem to demonstrate the governing prudence to keep us out of war where possible and/or where war cannot really be won (or its cost is too high). But at the same time, innocent people must be defended and the good of peoples and societies must be preserved. The common good must be defended. The Catholic tradition has been a "just war" tradition, though recent decades have seen an increasing openness and even embrace of pacifism. But it must be recalled that the criteria for a just war were developed, in the first instance, not in order to justify going to war, but rather to restrain war in its origin and in its conduct. In fact, this presumption in favor of peace is implied by Aquinas's phrasing of the first article on war in the *ST*: "Whether it is always sinful to wage war?" (*ST* q. 40, art. 1).

When war must be waged, its direction requires a considerable "military" prudence. Recall that, for Aquinas, the virtue of prudence aims at the good, not simply at the most effective and efficient. Prudence is not simply about efficient strategies to attain any desired end. For its part, military prudence is not simply about how to defeat an enemy effectively and efficiently. A general could be a brilliant strategist in conducting war but lack the virtue of military prudence by which he or she would consider the moral ramifications of planned strategies. As a virtue, military prudence must seek not only efficiency and effectiveness (which obviously are not irrelevant), but also the true good of the impacted parties, including the innocent, as well as the consequences of different courses of action which might be effective but more costly to human life and society—which can be an especially difficult thing in time of war and violence.

Virtues Related to Prudence

All of the cardinal virtues of prudence, justice, fortitude, and temperance are "hinge" virtues, which means that all of the other moral virtues are related in some way to these four. In his discussion of each of the cardinal virtues, then, in addition to specific types of a particular virtue, Aquinas also identifies other related (or auxiliary) virtues. His teaching on the virtues related to prudence is the briefest, and he clearly sees these virtues very much at the service of prudence. Specifically, Aquinas identifies the virtues related to prudence by their Greek names as *eubulia*, *synesis*, and *gnome* (which have proven difficult to translate into equivalent English terms).

Eubulia is the virtue that inclines us to seek sound information and good counsel. Not everyone is inclined to do so—for a variety of possible reasons, such as a tendency to make overly hasty judgments or forms of self-deception that subtly move a person to avoid discovering information or counsel that might direct them away from the right course of action. *Eubulia* is clearly necessary for a prudent decision, and yet it is possible for one to seek out good advice and still not prudently put it into action. Some people do regularly seek counsel, but remain too cautious or timid to act when necessary. *Eubulia*, then, is a habitual disposition that serves prudence; but it is not yet prudence, since one does not necessarily and habitually incorporate the information and counsel one has sought.

Synesis is the abiding inclination to make good practical judgments about the information that we receive and about options under consideration. Not everyone who seeks good advice can, in the end, sort out good counsel from bad or sound information from faulty. *Synesis* too, then, is a virtue that is auxiliary to prudence, but it is not yet prudence.

The virtue of *gnome* is perhaps the most interesting in that it shows Aquinas's recognition of the real complexity of situations and the impossibility of rules and laws covering every possible situation. *Gnome* is the virtue by which one makes a good decision when common principles or rules do not seem to apply. Extraordinary situations call for a distinct kind of virtue, a more discriminating kind of judgment than the virtue of *synesis*. *Gnome* is the virtue for recognizing and applying yet higher principles in extraordinary cases. While, for example, justice demands that we return to people what legitimately belongs to them, *gnome* would enable us to see that we must not do so if we have reason to believe that the person intends to do serious harm to the innocent with the return of his or her property. This is clearly a more discriminating unfolding of prudence.

In this sense, *gnome*, in its relation to prudence functions is like the virtue of *epikeia* in its relation to the virtue of justice (II-II, q.120). *Epikeia* enables us to make a sound judgment that retains sincere respect for law while recognizing that a particular rule or norm was not meant to apply to every particular situation—that is, if those who made the law were present, they would agree that the law was not meant to apply to this particular situation. For Aquinas, both *gnome* in relation to prudence and *epikeia* in relation to justice exist within a fundamental presupposition of the importance and validity of laws and rules, even as they recognize that the complexity of actual situations cannot be fully encompassed by those laws and rules. And it is precisely the central virtue of prudence and its auxiliary virtues which allow those who sincerely seek the good to maneuver through such complexity.

The Vice of Imprudence

As we have seen, every virtue has its contrary, and the obvious contrary of prudence is imprudence. This vice is defined especially by the absence of those things that characterize the virtue of prudence. Imprudent people have an abiding tendency to make hasty, poorly considered decisions, without having sought proper counsel. Or, on the other hand, they fail to act rightly in a timely manner because their deliberation goes on and on. They might be overly cautious and slow to act when the best possible realization of the good demands more prompt action. These, then, are the two modes of imprudence: either in the form of negligence or irresoluteness.

Imprudence can manifest itself in the form of rushing to decision and action. The imprudent person fails to take the time and effort to ascertain what is really going on in a particular situation, who and what is involved and what is at stake, what principles might help to guide a decision, and/or what persons or other resources could offer information or counsel. The imprudent decisions which result, therefore, will flow necessarily from superficial or even purely subjective judgments or values.

On the other hand, imprudence can also consist of a failure to make a decision or to move forward with a decision already made. As we have seen, Aquinas sees many essential elements to the virtue of prudence and therefore, by extension, to good decision-making. But it would be wrong to think that Aquinas is suggesting that decisions and action should be delayed as long as possible. In fact, some situations demand quick responses. Sometimes, hesitation is the correct response in order to re-evaluate or gather new information. But the unwillingness to make a decision that must be made, the endless review of information and the gathering of yet more data, continuing to go back and forth with possible options already duly considered, and being irresolute in carrying out what has been judged to be a good decision, is a manifestation of imprudence. Again, as we have seen, virtues enable us to act "with ease, smoothness, and promptitude." Some decisions are, in fact, complex and difficult even for the person of prudence; however, refusing to make a decision that must be made or failing to carry it out is not prudence, but overcaution and imprudence.

Just as, for Aquinas, every virtue is necessarily prudent, so too every vice and sin has an essential element of imprudence. The intemperate person acts without prudence in regard to the objects of his or her disordered desires. Such people may too readily place themselves in situations and circumstances in which they should know that their desire will overpower their right judgment. The unjust person shows imprudence in dealing with what legitimately is owed to another. He or she might set out to defraud or cheat—or it may be the case that the failure which leads to injustice is the imprudence of inadequate consideration of the whole situation. The cowardly or foolhardy person is imprudent in regard to an obstacle that must be confronted in order to attain a good. This is perhaps clearest in the person who imprudently rushes into danger without adequately weighing the risks in light of the good to be obtained or by failing to take available time to think through other possible options or safer courses of action.

Imperfect or Counterfeit Forms of Prudence

Imprudence involves the absence of one or more of the essential elements of prudence. Still, there can be a kind of imperfect prudence in which one or more of the elements is not fully present or fully utilized. The formation of a moral virtue takes time and practice, and one can fail to be fully prudent without being truly imprudent. In such cases, there is a defect in or an absence of some element of prudence. This is similar to Aquinas's teaching about the imperfect virtue of continence. It is not yet the ability to act chastely with ease, smoothness, and promptitude; but the fact that the continent person can habitually refrain from unchaste actions—even though with some inner struggle—is a step in the right direction.

There is a kind of imperfect prudence that aims at something which is not bad, but is not directed to what is ultimately good for authentic human fulfillment. For example, there can be a kind of imperfect prudence involved in running a business effectively. As long as one is not motivated principally or solely by selfish ends or unjust in attaining them, such effective practical decision-making is not bad. At one level, it is good and can reap benefits for the person, employees, stockholders, and others. It is not imprudence, nor is it merely a counterfeit of prudence. But since it is not directed to the true and whole good of the person, it can only be called a kind of imperfect prudence.

Aquinas speaks too of false or counterfeit forms of prudence—the ability to pursue goals efficiently and effectively, which may look like prudence at work, but is not. As we have said, one of the most essential characteristics of any and all virtue is that it aims at the good. Any ability, aptitude, or abiding tendency that is not aimed at the good cannot be a virtue. On a larger scale, if a person's life as a whole, is aimed at merely selfish or worldly ends, that person cannot truly be prudent, even if he or she appears to be.

In essence, false or counterfeit prudence has the appearance of prudence, but it involves seeking a bad end (or using inappropriate means to attain even a good end). A person might be effective at raising money for a charitable organization—but, done for the sake of a selfish end, such as merely to win human praise or vainglory, it is really a counterfeit of prudence. In the same way, someone who uses shady means in effectively raising money for a charity—such as dubious forms of investments—is exercising a counterfeit form of prudence, even though his or her overall intention might be good and sincere. Prudence seeks the good by good means. In this latter example, imprudence is linked to injustice.

In addressing false prudence, Aquinas mentions in particular what he calls "craftiness." This is the planning by deceitful or cunning ways to get something done. When this planning takes shape in action, Aquinas calls it "guile" or "fraud." We might also call it "cheating." Someone working as a fundraiser for a reputable not-for-profit organization might be highly effective in his or her work. This may seem like a kind of prudence, in serving a good in which this fundraiser sincerely believes—or at least a kind of imperfect prudence if the person is really "just making a living" in a form of effective promotion or sales. But this same person would be crafty in thinking of shifty or dishonest ways to attain the authentic good that the not-for-profit serves. And, acting on such plans through means like less-than-honest presentations of the institution's resources or activities, he or she would be acting with guile, committing fraud, or cheating potential donors in attaining even a worthy goal.

Covetousness at the Root of Imprudence

At the end of his discussion of false forms of prudence, Aquinas offers a brief but truly insightful discussion about what he calls "covetousness" at its root. Josef Pieper draws out this insight in his classic work *The Four Cardinal Virtues*.

Covetousness, strictly speaking, is a vice contrary to justice and specifically to its allied virtue of liberality or generosity (II-II, q. 118). It involves an immoderate love of and striving after material possessions in the hopes of assuring a person of his or her status or importance. It is inherently selfish and unconcerned for the good of others; while justice, by its nature, is aimed at the good of others and of the community. Considering Aquinas's teaching that covetousness is the root of false forms of prudence, Pieper proposes that Aquinas is really suggesting a broader sense of covetousness. There is, Pieper notes, a kind of more generalized selfishness or striving after security and self-assurance that undermines truly good decision-making and the virtue of prudence itself.

All virtue, including prudence, must aim at the good, ultimately the good of our authentic fulfillment as human beings—our own and that of others. Selfish focus on ourselves can only get in the way of decisions to attain the good. Such selfishness could easily undermine our ability to size up a situation accurately if we suspect our own purposes or narrow good seem threatened. We might become blind to authentic principles or rules that might guide us to the right. We might fail to seek out or take to heart sound advice. Covetousness, conceived in this broader sense as a kind of excessive self-focus or self-serving, would undermine the functioning and formation of the virtue of prudence.

Perhaps this is even clearer and more potentially harmful when we speak of the other specific types of prudence, whether "domestic," "ruling," or "political" prudence. These other types of prudence, even more than its personal form, must take into account the common good of a community together with the good of its individual members. Any form of selfishness—whether covetousness in its strict form or as a more general self-serving—would obstruct such prudence. The decisions of spouses and parents legitimately take into account their own individual good, but such considerations cannot be overriding in relation to the good of others in the family or the family unit. A selfish concern to pursue one's own personal career goals could easily obstruct or distort decisions about the future of the family.

Prudent decisions cannot be made by political leaders who are primarily motivated by pleasing donors or insuring re-election for themselves. Public officials who do not take into account the good of all of those impacted by decisions cannot make prudent decisions. On the other hand, citizens cannot vote with the prudence appropriate to them if they can only see their own good and the good of their own families and regions.

In pastoral leadership, difficult decisions must sometimes be made: staff members must be challenged or even let go for the good of the community. But if a pastoral leader hates conflict so much that he or she cannot accept the responsibility of challenging others in a prudent way, the community cannot be well-served. In a similar way, the good of a community and its future may require, for example, fundraising to renovate a space, hire new staff, or purchase new items. But again, if the pastoral leader cannot rise above his or her reluctance to face the conflict that renovations can bring or aversion to asking for donations even for a worthy cause, then truly prudent decisions for the good of the community can easily be thwarted.

True prudence must be free of self-serving, for one's own sake and for the sake of those impacted by one's choices. This is no small challenge, since self-focus is part of the sinful human condition. At a human level, it requires a willingness to be self-critical about one's own motives and basic life motivations. It also demands an openness to the criticism and appraisals of others around us. Friends in particular can help us to see ourselves as we are with greater accuracy, even while friendship itself calls us out of selfishness into concern for another. Collaborative decision-making is an important tool in decisions for a family or community. But beyond these human helps, there is the ongoing work of conversion, grounded in the growth of a selfless love. Prudence, like all of the virtues, can only find its real fulfillment when shaped, guided, and empowered by love for God and love like God's, manifest in the selfless loving of Jesus.

3

Justice

(*ST* II-II, qq. 57–122)

THE VIRTUE OF JUSTICE, as understood by Saint Thomas Aquinas and the Catholic tradition, is grounded in the recognition that we are inherently related to other persons. We all live in a wide variety of relationships, in communities of different sizes and types, and in the broader societies to which we belong (and today in an ever increasingly globalized world society). These relationships are essential to who and what we are. To be human is to be relational and communal. To be fully human is to live well in relationship with others and in community. The virtue of justice regulates these multiple relations, insuring that with ease, smoothness, and promptness we are able to act rightly in regard to others and to our communities. Men and women of justice actively contribute to the common good of society and to healthy and respectful communities and relationships. Our own good as individuals—and not merely in practical ways—depends on the health of these interpersonal and communal associations. Our manner of contributing to them is critical to our authentic growth as human persons.

Today when we speak of justice, we are often referring to something like the current relative state of equality, fairness, or recognition of fundamental rights between persons and in society. Or we are focused on principles of justice, tenets by which we try to insure that rights are respected and proper equality is achieved. But Aquinas is focused more particularly on justice precisely as a virtue, as a habitual disposition or an acquired and abiding tendency that resides in people who live and act in the context of multiple relationships, social and interpersonal. His lengthy discussion of justice does include the elements or principles of a theory of justice, but he implies that none of that will have practical effect unless the virtue of justice dwells in the people who must act and seek proper relations in the world.

The virtue of justice is the abiding disposition to give to people what is owed to them, what is "their due"—again, not begrudgingly but with ease, smoothness, and promptness. In biblical terms, we might speak today of justice as "right relationships." Especially in the Old Testament, people are "just" to the degree that they are in right relationship with God and with others within the context of covenantal relations, respecting their obligations to all. But this is really Aquinas's point as well. The virtue of justice is the habitual disposition to live in right relationship with other persons (and, as we shall see, with God), respecting our obligations to other individuals and to the good of the communities to which we belong and from which we benefit.

Justice in a World of Individualism

The health of any relationship or community of any size depends on the active participation of its members, each one benefiting from their shared goods, but also contributing as necessary. This is obviously true, simply at a practical level. Every society needs some sense of justice—responsibility to others and to the group in general—in order to survive and flourish. People must both benefit and contribute, however that might be conceived and structured. But for Aquinas and for the Catholic tradition, the right to benefit and the responsibility to contribute is not simply a practical reality. It is also essential for the goodness and authenticity of each of the members. Each individual must have a disposition to give to others what is demanded by their relationship—for the sake of the others, but also and essentially in order to live in a truly human way.

The foundational Christian belief about the human person is that we are created in the image of God (Gen 1:26–27). We are stamped, as it were, with the image of a God who is love. Our creation is a fruit of the overflow of this divine love. But more, this God is a Triune God: One God in Three Persons. Our God is relational within the divine nature itself—an eternity of mutual giving and receiving in the heart of God. We who are created as the image of God (*imago dei*) are therefore made in the image of the Trinity (*imago trinitatis*). And this same God has destined us to share in the divine life for all eternity, together with all of those, like us, created in the divine image. All of this means that we are relational by nature; we are our best and truest selves in authentic relationships; and our destiny is also profoundly social—eternal life within the life of God together with our brothers and sisters. This is the theological and anthropological foundation of Saint Thomas's understanding of justice.

But our contemporary world is a world of individualism, and this reality has a tremendous impact on how we conceive justice, our responsibilities to others, and what it means to be in "right relations" with others. No one can doubt that we exist in multiple relationships which confer benefits on us. Simply at a practical level, we need other individuals, and we need society. But without a deeper sense of how these relationships actually constitute us as persons, it becomes more difficult to understand what justice truly is and why we would need a virtue that is focused on right relationships, beyond a basic sense of fairness and equality. From the perspective of a relational and social understanding of the human person, individualism is a true and sad diminishment of the human person and of the society in which human persons live.

In a world of sovereign, independent individuals, the great value must be sovereign freedom—and freedom, not as a positive capacity to be and become what God intends us to be, but as the unhindered ability of each person to decide as he or she wants. In this view, the only restraint on freedom should be some kind of implicit social agreement that we refrain from actively harming others by our otherwise completely free choosing. Without such a bare minimum of limits on freedom, we could not live together in society with any kind of security or practical commerce. What is justice in such a context? Sadly, it is too easily reduced to whatever ensures that my freedom is not unduly hindered and that others are not actively harmed by the exercise of someone else's freedom. But what an emaciated view of the individual, of society, of human freedom, and of justice!

To truly capture the wisdom of Aquinas in his discussion of justice, we must recapture a sense of ourselves as foundationally and constitutively in relationship with others in communities and societies. The health—the "rightness"—of such relations and our commitment to them constitute our own health as authentic human beings. I am diminished as a human person by relationships and membership in societies in which others are not respected and in which their rights and dignity are not acknowledged and honored. It is absolutely true that freedom is fundamental to our humanity, but true freedom is a freedom *for* good and *for* God, not simply freedom *from* restraint.

Types of Justice

Aquinas identifies several types of justice in keeping with the different types of relationships and communities in which we live. These principal types are commutative, legal, and distributive. The Catholic social tradition after Saint Thomas has greatly expanded on our understanding of these species of justice, but a great deal of subsequent reflection and teaching will build from this foundation.

At the individual level, justice involves the habitual disposition to recognize and respect the rights of other individuals, whether those are fundamental human rights like the right of self-determination (for example, in making medical decisions for themselves) or the claims that are based on our prior commitments to them such as contracts. At this individual level, Aquinas speaks of *commutative* justice. It involves the relationship of individual to individual and presupposes a fundamental equality between persons. In fact, for Aquinas, any form of injustice is implicitly a kind of failure to recognize this foundational equality: the unjust person withholds what belongs to another because of an implicit belief that he or she is more important, more worthy, etc. Just people in relation to other individuals respect the commitments that they have made, and they honor basic rights that are prior to any explicit agreement. A person of justice, for example, returns items that she borrowed at the agreed-upon time, provides the work or product for which she was duly paid, and respects the property and due privacy of her neighbors.

In relation to the larger group or society, the virtue of justice disposes the individual to contribute to the good of the community more broadly and thus to the benefit of all of its members. Aquinas called this *general* or *legal* justice—though by using this term, he was not restricting such justice to the matters included in civil law. It is "legal" in the sense that all law is directed to the common good—just as this type of justice is. In contemporary terms, this is also called *contributive* justice (or, for some, *social* justice). In justice, we have a duty to contribute to the good of the societies in which we live and from which we benefit. This is most clearly manifest in the responsibility to pay taxes, vote responsibly, and accept the military draft in time of just war. Again, for Aquinas, this is a type of virtue—an abiding tendency to attend to our duties to community and society.

Reciprocal with legal (or contributive) justice is what Saint Thomas calls *distributive* justice. Just as individuals have the duty to contribute to the common good, they also have the right to benefit from the common good. Social welfare systems are one obvious example of a societal, systemic way to try to insure such just distribution. Precisely as a virtue, distributive justice is the abiding tendency to insure a just sharing of societal goods. The person of distributive justice, then, accepts the right of less fortunate individuals to receive their fair share of societal benefits. In our age, this usually involves support for prudent legal and structural means to ensure such distribution to those whose rightful share in the common good is threatened by poverty, discrimination, or the like.

Justice and the Wider Web of Our Relationships

It is clearer to us today that we must live as well in right relationship with the earth and with the rest of the created order. Human persons are uniquely created in the image of God, but we remain part of the created order and dependent on it in fundamental ways. We are responsible to care for it as stewards. Since we all share in the natural resources of this earth—we ourselves and people throughout the world and throughout history—our responsibility for the earth is, at the same time and more properly, a matter of justice to other persons. We must cultivate within ourselves the habitual tendency to act responsibly toward the earth and thus toward others who do, should, or will share in its resources. Pope Francis has made this responsibility abundantly clear in his encyclical letter, *Laudato si'*.

We must also live in right relationship with ourselves—that is, respecting our own legitimate rights, needs, aspirations, and responsibilities. For Aquinas, this would be a kind of justice by analogy to the properly other-directed nature of justice. But he was quite aware that we have a moral responsibility to care for our own spiritual and physical well-being. Even as we care for others in work and ministry, we must care also for ourselves. Jesus said that we must love our neighbor *as ourselves*. We must be just with others—*and* with ourselves. This does not deny or negate the fact that Christian love, after the model of Jesus, is other-directed and self-giving; it simply affirms (at the very least) the practical reality that if we don't care for ourselves, we will have very little to give others.

Justice is about our obligations and duties to others. In truly personal interrelationships—relationships meant to be characterized by love—such as marriage, family, and close friendship, categories of strict justice do not perfectly fit. We will look more closely below at the virtues related to justice that focus on such relationships. And yet, it is helpful in this context to acknowledge that in every relationship, there is the necessity of possessing and nurturing an abiding tendency to give to others what we owe them even if they are not matters of quantifiable or even strict obligations. Spouses who do not give quality time to one another—or parents to their children or one friend to another—are, in a real sense, being unjust to them, even though the time rightfully expected by spouses, children, and elderly parents is not quantifiable. Respecting one another, attending to one another, listening to one another may not constitute quantifiable obligations or be entirely analogous to the contractual arrangements that can be the subject of commutative justice, but we owe such things to one another. Without justice, there cannot be love. We cannot claim to love someone if we do not give him or her what we owe.

Justice and Other Virtues

Justice must characterize all of our other virtues. The considerations of prudence must remain cognizant of our relations with and responsibilities to others. The prudent person cannot make decisions based solely on the consideration of what is good for him or her alone. The prudent choice, in end and means, is attentive to its impact on other people. The exercise of courage must encompass a willingness to face obstacles for the good of others, recognizing that we are inherently related to them—even if they are strangers to us. The truly courageous person is not a lone ranger, but someone willing to sacrifice for others and attentive to how his or her actions will impact others. The temperate person seeks not only an inner balance and harmony, but also its outward manifestation in relation to others. Perhaps we might think of chastity, one form of temperance, also as an exercise in justice—a matter of the respect for other people, not only in our actions but also in our thoughts and fantasies.

The Vice of Injustice

As the contrary of the virtue of justice, the vice of injustice is the acquired disposition to withhold what is due to other individuals or to the communities to which we belong and from which we benefit. It is a failure to live in right relationship with others as a matter of acquired habit. And, as we have seen, it is implicitly a failure to recognize our fundamental equality with other persons by denying them what we would expect for ourselves.

Aquinas discusses obvious and glaring forms of injustice such as murder, robbery and theft, bodily harm, cheating and fraud, and false accusations. But forms of the vice of injustice exist too in more ordinary circumstances, closer to home than we might commonly ponder. In fact, Aquinas considers *harsh judgment* of others to be a form of injustice. We owe it to the people around us to presume good of them and give them the benefit of the doubt until there is some clear reason to think otherwise. To think ill of others without good reason, based only on suspicions, is an injustice. We commonly call this being judgmental—and it can sadly become an abiding tendency in our perspective toward those around us.

It is unjust, says Aquinas, to show respect or grant privileges to some and not to others for selfish or trivial reasons. This is traditionally called being a "respecter of persons"—not, in this case, in the sense of showing an authentic respect for the people involved, but rather making an unjust discrimination between persons. Showing preference to friends, relatives, the wealthy, or the attractive in situations where objectivity is demanded is a form of injustice to others. This would be especially evident in a judge or the like, but it is also possible to give one's time or attention to one person while neglecting someone with greater claim on it. In the New Testament, James illustrates this form of injustice when he condemns Christians who invite the wealthy to take seats of honor in the assembly while calling the poor to stand or sit on the floor (James 2:2–3).

Beyond unjust tendencies in thought, Aquinas provides an insightful identification of forms of injustice in word—again, not only as occasional actions, but as acquired dispositions. Words can sometimes be trivial in their impact on others; at other times, they are not. The rightness of basic human relations, which is the concern of justice, can be seriously undermined by types of speech that tear down others or treat them with contempt or scorn. The tendency to speak ill of others who are not present ("backbiting"), whether one is speaking the truth or not, is a form of the vice of injustice. It is "detraction" to speak a truth that brings dishonor to another person without good reason or not in the right circumstances and to the right people. Aquinas tells us that willingly listening to such talk shares in its guilt. There are, in fact, people who have a tendency to tear others down in speech; and there are others who may not tend to the talking but delight in the hearing. The propensity to gossip brings harm to others, and tale-bearing stirs up trouble. Aquinas notes that, since friends are one of life's most precious possessions, the tendency to stir up trouble between or among friends through gossip and the like is a serious injustice. While teasing and banter among friends can be innocent enough, the disposition to make fun of others or belittle them is a vice opposed to justice. Wishing others harm in thought and word too is unjust.

We can probably all identify to some degree with these injustices in speech. Hopefully, they are occasional slips or bad judgments. But we know that we can all find ourselves easily enough with an abiding tendency to judge others harshly, to savor and spread gossip about others, to tear others down in speech, or to use forms of humor that, in fact, undermine good relationships with others. Such behaviors and abiding attitudes harm ourselves as the agents who harbor and foster such habits; they injure the "victims" of our words; and they damage the health of the networks of relationships in which we live and upon which we all depend.

Virtues Related to Justice

The virtues related to justice share its focus on the authentic health of our relationships and communities. But some virtues, such as piety and religion which concern our responsibility to parents and to God, involve duties to others which can never be fully met. (Aquinas devotes quite a bit of attention to these two virtues, so we will examine them in larger sections below.) Others do not involve strict obligations as such that can be quantified or measured but which nonetheless are attitudes necessary for healthy relations and communities.

Truth-telling

Truth-telling, or honesty, is simply essential to good relationships and good communities. We cannot live together in harmony if, at a fundamental level, we cannot presume that the speech that passes between and among us will be fundamentally honest. This is immediately obvious in marriages and friendships which can easily be torn apart by lies. But it is also true of our life in communities and in society. Even something as basic as economic exchanges depend on truth-telling.

Once again, of course, Aquinas is speaking especially of honesty as a virtue—an abiding tendency to tell the truth that we build up over time, one choice after another. We may know from sad experience, on the other hand, that the vice of dishonesty grows easily enough, one "little white lie" after another, until we find it difficult to speak the truth when it deserves to be told. It does not require active malice to build up a vice. Often enough, a little variation from the truth may seem like a convenient decision in the moment—to save ourselves, for example, from embarrassment or awkwardness. But, over time, this undermines our ability at critical moments to speak the truth. It becomes all too easy to seek the path of least resistance by telling a "harmless, little" lie.

Honesty is obviously opposed by lying and the vice of dishonesty, which is the abiding tendency to say things intentionally that aren't true. Lying in words has its parallel too in ways of acting. Aquinas tells us that *dissimulation* is the attempt to give a false appearance or to be seen in a false light. I might, for example, feign interest in or concern for someone's problems when my purpose is simply to draw close enough to that person in order to gain some knowledge or advantage. A transcript of our conversation might not show a single spoken lie, but my feigned sympathy is itself a lie in action. We would likely call a person with the vice of dissimulation a "fake."

Hypocrisy is one of the principal forms of dissimulation in which, more specifically, one tries to appear nobler, wiser, or holier than one is. *Boasting* is presenting oneself as better than you are, a kind of self-praise. This would be, for example, a braggart who exaggerates his or her accomplishments or abilities. On the other hand, "irony" in Aquinas's distinctive terms is a kind of false or feigned humility by which one presents oneself as less than one truly is. In this way, someone might be prone to avoid responsibilities that the person is, in fact, capable of accomplishing, or one might be feigning humility as a kind of hypocritical show of virtue.

Interpersonal and Domestic Virtues

There are, according to Aquinas, other more "homey" sorts of virtues that we might not normally associate with justice, but which we can easily recognize as essential to good human living and sorely missed when they are absent. Individuals who lack them do not contribute well to the interrelational and communal contexts in which they find themselves. Again, these may not be quantifiable as strict obligations, but they are nonetheless necessary for good relationships and communities—and for becoming authentically good members of those relationships and communities. Such virtues are concerned with what we might call an attitude of "civility"—a term related to the words "civic," "civilization," "civilized," and "citizenship"—all from a Greek word that refers to the common life in the "city." These "virtues of civility" make us positive and contributing members of life in the city/community.

Vengeance

One such related virtue is traditionally translated by the unfortunate term "vengeance"—which doesn't sound like much of a virtue at all. It involves measured retribution or expectation of compensation. When we look at the virtue of temperance, we will see that anger directed against a genuine evil can be appropriate and even good since it moves us to oppose evil. Still, anger must be properly moderated by reason. In the realm of justice, when someone has committed a wrong or acted unjustly, the effected persons can rightfully expect due compensation. Reciprocally, the offending person has an obligation to provide restitution. In this sense, criminals who violate the law (based in justice) have a duty to "pay the price" for their injustice to harmed individuals and to the common good of society. But such retribution, like "good" anger, must be moderated by reason—and this is the function of the virtue of "vengeance" or measured recompense.

We might tell ourselves immediately that this talk of moderated retribution does not speak to our ordinary existence. But that's not true. There are people who easily "fly off the handle" if they believe that others have spoken ill of them, belittled them, or spread tales about them. As we have seen, these would be offenses against justice; and, if the person's perception is accurate, he or she is due proper "restitution" (e.g., having the truth told, untruths retracted, or apologies given). But the offended person's response could be disproportionate to the actual harm done. There are people who have a habit of "making a mountain out of a mole hill." They would need to work on the virtue unfortunately named "vengeance." Its absence clearly undermines good relationships.

Closer yet to home are the virtues of thankfulness (gratitude), friendliness (affability), and liberality (generosity). And then there is another unusual virtue traditionally called *epikeia* (equity). Most of these (except the last) would probably fall under the broader title of courtesy—not in the sense of highbrow manners or social fussiness, but more like the oil that keeps the social machine chugging along easily and smoothly. Relationships and communities are about people—flesh-and-blood human persons with feelings and felt responses for good or ill. These relationships can't operate well—really, they can't operate *humanly*—without virtues like thankfulness, affability, and generosity.

Thankfulness

We all know people who live their lives in a spirit of gratitude. They are grateful to God for divine favors, even in the midst of hardships. They are quick to recognize a favor or a kindness done to them. They are quick with a sincere thanks and perhaps even a (these days, rare) thank-you note. The virtue of thankfulness or gratitude is the abiding tendency to be aware of favors done and gifts given and to respond in appropriate ways. On the other hand, it is equally possible to lack this disposition all together. There are people who never seem to notice kindnesses shown them or never appear to feel any obligation to offer a word of thanks or a favor in return. Such people without the virtue of gratitude can be an irritation in relationships and in communities.

Gratitude is not a matter of strict obligation, as justice is. It concerns favors done and gifts freely given. Thankfulness is not really owed if two parties in a contract both observe their ends of the bargain—unless one party freely goes over and above what is expected. The checkout clerk at the market is paid to scan my purchases and take my cash. "Thank you" might be my habitual response upon receiving the receipt, but I really have no reason to be grateful unless the clerk was particularly kind or helpful, or unless I presented a problem "over and above" the call of duty. And yet, even without being a strict obligation in justice, there is a real way that we nonetheless owe something to people who are kind to us—"owe," not necessarily in a tangible way (though perhaps so), but a response of the heart or in attitude and gesture (e.g., a "simple" thank-you).

Again, gratitude is not a matter of strict obligation. Trying to calculate the price of every gift given so that you can immediately respond with a "gift" of the precise, same value is not gratitude. This kind of tit-for-tat thinking seeks to dissolve the kind of dependence that gratefully receiving a gift should bring. Moreover, sometimes greater gratitude is owed to someone who gave something of little tangible value but that flows from a more generous intention or desire. Still, although gratitude is not a strict obligation in justice, properly speaking, this does not mean that a response is not called for: a thank-you, a prayer raised up for the benefactor, or even a resolve to give a gift in the future. "I owe you one" is not an inappropriate response, as long as it does not mean that the original gift has been reduced to its monetary value or precise level of effort.

Healthy friendships, marriages, and familial relationships are nurtured by people with the virtue of gratitude. Lack of gratitude can hurt, offend, and sap the life out of such relationships. Thankfulness is also an obligation in our relationship with God. Fostering it by regularly recalling how blessed we are is essential to the spiritual life. But a spirit of gratitude to generous employers, reliable coworkers, affable store clerks, helpful law enforcement officers, and the like are also obligations. Such an attitude—being attentive to the assistance and kindness of others—makes us better human beings and encourages us to "pay it forward." It may not be an absolute require- ment for the efficient operation of a community, but it is the oil that makes it more satisfying, more comfortable, and just more human.

Friendliness or Affability

If you have ever had to work, live, or eat with grouchy, dour, or sullen people, you know immediately the importance of the virtue of affability or friendliness. Having to face an ill-natured coworker, a sullen bank teller, or a sulking teenager across a desk or a breakfast table can wear on anyone's previously cheery day. On the other hand, we all know how simple, ordi- nary interactions and even difficult moments can be lightened by a smile, a little warmth, or a pleasant demeanor. It is true that we are not speaking here about matters of dire oppression or what causes wars and civil strife. But these are matters that make interactions more pleasing, and again more human. One doesn't have to make friends with everyone else, but one should live with others in a manner that is amiable and pleasant.

People who have an abiding tendency to be surly, sullen, contrary, or quarrelsome are a weight on the people around them and sadly seem themselves to be unfortunate human beings. On the other hand, people who have the habitual disposition to be pleasant and warm—not in an in- sincere or merely superficial way (which could be the vice that Aquinas calls "flattery")—make social interactions enjoyable and community life more personable. Someone with this virtue can maintain their affability with ease and smoothness, even when experiencing their own inconve- niences or difficulties. Again, think about the reaction of various people in a delayed checkout line in a store, airport security checkpoint, or in line to be rebooked for a canceled flight. Some people can easily become irate and rude to clerks or agents who have no control over the situation, causing a scene or making a difficult situation even more unpleasant for the people around them. At the same time, other people, equally inconvenienced, can maintain a spirit of good-humor that can calm and even cheer those around them. What a blessing to human living to be surrounded by affable and friendly people!

Liberality or Generosity

Imagine a world in which people only gave to one another what was strictly owed to them and not a single iota more. Generosity or liberality is the virtue that gives beyond what is required. It is related to the virtue of justice in that it concerns giving to others, but it exceeds what justice strictly demands. Aquinas tells us that *liberality*, in the first instance, concerns money, and it manifests a relative freedom from excessive concern about it. But *generosity* with one's money reveals a deeper disposition of giving that manifests itself in freely giving time, attention, praise, one's energy and talents, and more. There is often something particularly attractive about truly generous people—most probably because they manifest a trait that is authentically human. In faith terms, God is over-the-top in generosity; and, created in the divine image, we are most truly ourselves in imitating such willingness to give. How pleasant it is to encounter a person who is free with sincere affirmation and praise.

When it comes to vices opposed to virtues, one can err by defect or by excess. *Covetousness* (avarice or greediness) is opposed to liberality by defect. Greedy people want to accumulate and keep rather than give. Again, while we might usually think of this vice in terms of money, there are people who are greedy about their time, their talents, and their giving of praise. They are unwilling to lend a hand even though they have the time and talent to be of assistance. By excess, we have the vice of *prodigality* or dissipation, which is the disposition to be immoderate or excessive in giving. The prodigal person gives beyond their means. The Gospel parable of the Prodigal Son (Luke 15:11–32) is the story of a young man who foolishly spends his inheritance on loose living. But the parable is also sometimes called the Parable of the Prodigal Father because the father (and by implication, God) is lavish and excessive in his offer of loving forgiveness.

Covetousness and prodigality remind us that all the other virtues, including generosity, must be guided by prudence.

Epikeia (A Justice That Is Prudent)

Another virtue, certainly less well-known and a bit obscure, is usually called by its Greek name *epikeia*. It concerns especially the manner of applying laws and other norms, and it's for this reason that Aquinas sees it as related to justice. Human laws simply cannot encompass every possible situation. They remain by necessity general. *Epikeia* is the habitual disposition to be able to discern if a particular law really applies in a particular case. It seeks justice and the common good when it is not clear that an existing law can do so in a particular case. Traditionally, *epikeia* asks the question "What was the original intent of this law, and was it really meant to apply to a situation like the one we have before us?" Clearly, *epikeia* represents, even more than usual, the interplay of the virtues of justice and prudence.

These days, *epikeia* is still invoked in some discussions of canon law and moral theology. It is a bit delicate, since it can seem to suggest that we can regularly "discern" that laws were not meant to apply to me. This is certainly not what Aquinas intended. In any case, although defining it precisely and understanding how it might work in actual situations is tricky, this particular virtue manifests the reality that laws and norms cannot always apply to each and every situation. Sometimes, the well-formed conscience and prudence (and *epikeia*) must simply do their very best.

Religion

One of the most interesting virtues that Aquinas understands to be related to justice is something that we probably do not commonly think to be a matter of virtue at all. It is the virtue of religion. As a virtue, it is the abiding tendency to give to God the honor, worship, and thanksgiving that we owe. It is the element of debt or obligation that relates it to justice; but religion is not simply a type of justice, since our debt to God can never be satisfied. How could we ever really give God adequate return for our creation, redemption in Christ, hope for eternal life, and all of the countless blessings that God has showered on us?

Our relationship with God, of course, cannot be reduced to matters of obligation. This is evident in the fact that even our human relationships with friends, spouses, and parents cannot be reduced to strict debts to be repaid in justice. With a completely gratuitous love, God gives us the theological virtues of faith, hope, and love in order to know God, expect to attain divine union, and enter into divine friendship. The virtue of religion, related to justice, is clearly akin to such supernatural virtues; but, as an acquired moral virtue, it is focused more particularly on the sense of obligation that human persons ought to have in relation to God, who has done so much for them. The theological virtues are focused on God directly and bring us into encounter with God; the moral virtue of religion remains focused on what human persons can and should do in acknowledging their debt to God. The virtue of religion, considered on its own, makes us better people in relation to God; the theological virtues make us holy.

Religion is the virtue by which we tend to give God what we owe. Like all of the moral virtues, it is directed to actions. In addressing the virtue, Aquinas speaks of the "acts" of religion. Because we are spirit and body, these acts are both internal and external. Interiorly, the virtue of religion expresses itself (and grows) by the religious acts of devotion and prayer.

Devotion in this context includes its more common meaning of the sincere feelings of adherence to God; but more fundamentally devotion is the interior will to give oneself increasingly to the service of God. Spiritual feelings may come and go, but the virtue of religion is realized in decisions and actions that express our service of God, regardless of our feelings at any particular moment. Perhaps we might "feel" like we don't want to go to church or "feel" like we aren't "getting anything out of it," but true devotion is an act of the will to give to God the time and the worship that God deserves. At the same time, recalling God's love for us and the divine mercy toward us can foster deeper feelings of devotion, which then can further fill and empower our devoted acts.

Prayer is also an interior act of the virtue of religion. It can manifest itself in external actions, but fundamentally it is interior. Anyone who has seriously tried to pray knows that if prayer depended on our feelings alone, we wouldn't be doing it faithfully for very long. Making and keeping the time for prayer—like making and keeping time for one's friends and family—is important even if we don't feel like it. It is an expression of our recognition of what God has given us. The more that we are aware of what God has done and is doing, the more we can recognize that we owe to God the time that we can set aside for prayer. Prayer is deeper than obligations and repaying of debts, but it is at least that. It is, miraculously, God who first wants to communicate and share with us. Prayer, at this level, is the living out of our responsibility to respond.

The external acts of religion generally concern more outward actions; but, done well, they involve inward attitudes as well. For Aquinas, such acts are adoration, sacrifice, tithing, and generous giving. Here we are focusing on the moral virtue of religion and its external acts. But it's important to see that Aquinas is really imagining that these religious acts will, of course, be filled, empowered, and directed by grace and more particularly by faith, hope, and love into a deepening personal relationship and ultimately union with God.

Pondering our relationship with God through the lens of justice and obligations may seem a bit odd or even off-putting. But recall that love requires justice. We cannot really claim that we love others if we fail to give them what we owe them. How authentic is our love for someone if, at a more basic level, we don't give them the respect that we owe them as persons? The interrelationship of love and justice points to the essential connection between love of God and our religious obligation to God. Love certainly cannot be reduced to justice—just as love of God cannot be reduced to religious acts and a "habitual disposition" to return to God, as best we can, some measure of what God has given us so abundantly. It is true that love cannot be reduced to justice, but love cannot exist without justice—just as love of God cannot exist with the religious acts by which we try to offer a response to God. In the same way, it is one thing to say "I love you" or to feel a warm and cozy affection for someone—it is quite another thing to make time for them, make sacrifices for them, and attend to them in themselves. It is empty to say that "I love God" without the resolve and disposition to do what is so evident in our relationship to other human persons: to make time, sacrifice for, and attend to.

In the spiritual life, it is all too easy to reduce everything to feelings—feeling God's presence, having good prayer experiences, feeling affirmed and uplifted by God. Often enough in our day, God is reduced to a doting grandparent figure who just wants to spoil us with whatever we want and who absentmindedly overlooks everything. In this context, it is easy to think that we can "take or leave" religious practices if they don't give us good feelings or if we don't feel like doing them. In this context, what Aquinas has to say about the virtue of religion in its relation to justice is a useful and important corrective. God is not a divine accountant keeping track of our obligations. God doesn't need our religion. We need our religion. To be authentically human is to give a return to God for what God has done for us, not only in thought but in action. God deserves it, and we need it.

Piety

Justice and its related virtues are concerned with right relationships. Piety is the virtue by which we tend habitually to give due honor and respect to those persons who in fact hold an important place in our lives, and who have benefited us in essential ways—most especially our parents. It's not a common phrase in our day, but we know that "filial piety" is respect and care for our parents. Beyond our parents, piety extends out to other important members of our families, especially our elders, but also to one's government and leaders of society and church.

We live in a time and culture substantially different from that of Aquinas. Family structures and dynamics are different. Citizens in a modern democracy have a different view of their relationship to their political leaders than their counterparts in hierarchically-ordered late medieval monarchies. Even in the Catholic Church, after the Second Vatican Council, we have a different way of relating to priests, bishops, and even the pope. Still, while acknowledging the differences in outlook, Aquinas's teaching on the virtue of piety can still offer us valuable insights for us today.

Our society has grown more informal in dress and manners of addressing others. It is sometimes startling to be called by one's first name by a very young store clerk who is reading our name on a credit card or computer screen. Government officials, political and religious leaders, professors, and others who hold important positions in society are no longer greeted with the same level of respect and honor. There is nothing inherently wrong with such things. They are largely matters of ever-changing cultural expectations. At the same time, marks of respect appropriate to a culture reinforce and acknowledge the distinctive value of the leadership and service that some people offer to a community, their unique accomplishments, or distinctive contributions. This is not to deny the fundamental dignity and equality of all persons, nor is it to encourage elitism or the promotion of pride and arrogance in a distinguished few. It is simply to say that we owe gratitude and respect to those who serve and lead us—which is no small task—and whose work contributes in a special way to our common good. It is a virtue to habitually tend to be aware and show such respect.

Filial Piety

None of us had perfect parents. If we are parents, none of us is a perfect parent. And still—except perhaps in cases of abuse, serious neglect, or abandonment—we all generally instinctually feel a responsibility to and for our parents. It would probably be difficult to feel otherwise in light of the many years that we lived under their authority and guiding hand. And, of course, hopefully there is always the memory of the love that our parents have shown over the years (even if imperfectly) and the sacrifices they have made for us. Again, piety is not justice, strictly speaking, but it recognizes the obligations that we have to those who have brought us into the world, cared for and nurtured us, and set us on our feet eventually to set out on our own. This debt is not measurable. Or to say it another way, it is incalculable.

As adults, we continue to listen respectfully to our parents' advice, even when unsolicited. There are ways of speaking to our friends and other family members that we would never use in addressing our parents. As they age and weaken in body and mind, we strive to exercise patience and attend to their needs, as best we can. In our day, often with no large network of extended families, adult children face the task of caring for their elderly parents in the midst of the busyness of their own work and family responsibilities. This can be a very difficult and even burdensome (but not uncommon) challenge.

Filial piety is a virtue—which means that it brings ease, smoothness, and promptness in doing the good. This is not to say that the actual care of frail parents becomes easy in itself, nor does it say that we can't feel reluctance from day to day. But the virtue enables us to move forward when we might otherwise turn back from a responsibility which is, in fact, reasonably in our power to meet. It helps us to see that we have a responsibility, empowers us to accept it, and keeps our sadness and reluctance from getting the best of us.

Again and again, we must note that every virtue must be guided by prudence. We all have multiple responsibilities and limited resources. Filial piety must be prudent. There are times when we cannot offer the assistance that we would want, because we have, for example, responsibilities to our own spouses and children. They need our time, attention, and financial resources too. (At the same time, my spouse should feel some level of filial piety and duty for his/her in-laws, as my children should for their grandparents.) Sometimes, elderly parents simply cannot be cared for at home. And, at some level, it is unjust for parents to expect their adult children to neglect other important responsibilities to attend to them. Those to whom piety is directed have a responsibility to strive to remain worthy of the honor and respect given them.

Patriotism and Piety

In general, we all accept the fact that citizens must pay reasonable taxes to support the government in its operations on behalf of the common good. Most people recognize that citizens should accept the draft to military service in time of war and threat to the nation. While many do not observe it, most would probably recognize some responsibility to keep abreast of current issues that impact our nation and society and then to vote in elections responsibly. These are, in fact, as we have seen, matters of strict justice.

The truth is that we owe something to the countries to which we belong. Our obligation is not simply the practical necessity of people who implicitly have bought into some kind of "social contract" by which we all agree to contribute to society in order to draw out benefits. Every citizen has benefited (sadly, some more than others) from the nation and society in which they have grown up. Our cultural self-identity, our sense of belonging, our values, and our worldview have been formed, for better and worse, by the societies and cultures in which we have been nourished. We have benefited from the resources that our nation makes available to us and the protections that it has provided. In the Catholic tradition, we see a deeper connectedness to those around us rooted in our very nature; but the reasons mentioned here alone remind us of the distinctive debt that we owe to our nation.

Patriotism seems to be a value that has waned in recent decades. Surely there are many reasons that we have less trust in our government and its leaders. A democracy cannot really flourish if respectful criticism and even active opposition to the government is met with the simple-minded "It's our country. Love it or leave it!" Still, something is lost in a society in which people don't have a love and respect for the country in which they were born and raised. And something is diminished in persons who do not foster in themselves the abiding attitude of thankfulness for what they have received from their country and a commitment to contribute to it, even when the contribution takes the form of sincere criticism.

Saint Thomas's teaching on the virtue of justice and its related virtues has a great deal to offer us in our age and society. In many ways, it challenges our presuppositions and the strength and depth of our sense of obligation to the people and communities around us. Aquinas reminds us of what we owe to our family and friends, to those with whom we work and whose neighborhoods we share, and to those who share our national and cultural heritage. In the contemporary world—certainly from the perspective of modern Catholic social thought—we see those interrelationships and communities and the realm of our responsibilities more broadly. If we want to live more truly human lives and contribute and benefit from a more human society, we would do well to reflect on the insights about justice and its related virtues offered to us by Saint Thomas Aquinas.

4

Fortitude (or Courage)

(*ST* II-II, qq. 123–40)

THE ENGLISH WORD "FORTITUDE" comes from a Latin root that means strong, steadfast, or sturdy. It is related to the English words "fort" and "fortified." The word "courage" derives from a Latin word that means "heart," and so it is related to the word "cardiology." In many cultures, the heart is a symbol for inner strength or determination. We might say, for example, that a young athlete "has a lot of heart," meaning that he or she is willing to work hard to achieve success. The words "fortitude" and "courage" are synonyms. They both refer to inner strength and steadfastness in the face of difficulties. We will use those words interchangeably here.

The virtue of fortitude is the abiding inclination to overcome obstacles or confront dangers to attain a good. It is the virtue that empowers soldiers, firefighters, and law-enforcement officials to confront the danger of death in order to defend innocent life and to serve the common good. No less courageous are doctors and nurses who volunteer to attend to people who face life-threatening epidemics such as Ebola or those who care for patients in dangerous warzones in faraway places. For Aquinas, it is the danger of losing the most basic good of our natural life—physical life itself—which characterizes fortitude in its most essential meaning. From a Christian perspective, it is the martyr who willingly faces death for the sake of the faith who displays the highest form of courage. In fact, Aquinas devotes an entire question in the *ST* to martyrdom in relation to courage (II-II, q. 124).

But the virtue of courage is not most often so extraordinary, so notably heroic. Life is full of obstacles, struggles, hardships, and difficulties that must be confronted in order to realize a good. It is a form of courage to give witness to one's faith by practicing it actively in the face of ridicule or subtle scorn. It is courageous to face difficult and burdensome medical treatments to preserve one's life, and especially to try to return to health for the sake of one's family. It takes fortitude to do what is right at work when one is pressured to do otherwise. It is a form of courage, too, to pursue one's education in face of other responsibilities and the need to work other jobs to pay tuition. It is courageous to keep one's head held high in the face of poverty and want, to continue to do what can and must be done, while at the same time refusing to let oneself be defeated emotionally and spiritually. In short, true courage is not some rare or necessarily extraordinary virtue. In fact, we need it in our ordinary human lives, which are rarely entirely free of struggle, difficulties, and obstacles.

Courage, says Aquinas, moderates fear. Fear, in itself, is not a bad thing. It is a natural response to the perception that some person, thing, or situation is a threat to us in some way. And so, fear can be a good thing. It is the recognition that we are, in fact, vulnerable and finite. But we must not allow ourselves to be ruled or paralyzed by fear. It's true that sometimes the prudent response to some danger is caution or retreat—or even running away at top speed. But, at the same time, there are some goods that are worthy of the challenges we must face in order to attain them. The firefighter should experience a prudent fear in the face of a building in flames, but he or she judges that the innocent lives to be saved are worth the risk. A married couple that decides to relocate to seek a better life is taking a risk, facing threat; but they may prudently and courageously decide that it is the best course of action in order to better provide for their children.

The virtue of courage is the sustained ability to recognize and accept our vulnerability to some danger, threat, or obstacle—our fear—but not be paralyzed by it. Courage does not necessarily eliminate fear—nor should it always do so, because there may be real danger worthy of the caution that fear brings. But courage is the ability to not be turned back or overcome by fear.

As a natural moral virtue, fortitude grows one choice after another. We become courageous in situations great and small by confronting one obstacle after another, by refusing to give up one time after another, by sticking with an effort despite its difficulty. Such effort, especially in the face of chronic or serious difficulties, can be aided (or sadly hindered) by those around us. The related words "encourage" and "discourage" point to our ability to help or hinder others in their growth in fortitude. To "en-courage" means literally to put or pour courage into another person. We can support the ability of others to face difficulties and to grow in this virtue by our words, our example, our support. On the other hand, we also have the power to "dis-courage"—literally to take courage away—by disparaging the efforts of others, by nay-saying their hopes, or by deflating their confidence. In justice and love, we owe others encouragement to face the challenges that confront them. And we owe it to others not to be a source of discouragement to them through our words, our example, or lack of the support that we might legitimately be able to give.

As is true for every virtue, fortitude requires a true desire to attain or accomplish an authentic good. It is the good to be attained that gives rise to the strength to face the obstacles that stand in the way. The recognition and appreciation of good calls forth the courage to obtain it. Cowardice, fortitude's contrary, is as much a failure to fully embrace a good worthy of pursuit as it is a failure to rise above one's fear. Because courage, like all of the virtues, is directed to the good, the ability to overcome difficulties in order to realize an evil end cannot be courage at all. The person who is willing to face grave danger in order to steal, to seek vengeance, or to harm the innocent is not courageous. Terrorists are not courageous, even if they are willing to blow themselves up. Courage aims at the authentically good—at worthy goals by worthy means.

Fortitude and Other Virtues

Aquinas notes that fortitude is often accompanied and even empowered by a kind of anger—anger in the sense of a felt determination to overcome. He discusses anger itself in relation to the virtue of temperance (II-II, q. 158) where he notes that not all anger is evil. It is in itself a passion, a power, to confront. The person facing cancer with courage is "going to beat it," "will not let herself be defeated by it," is willing to "fight it." A firefighter facing the flames can feel a surge of energy, which is a form of anger at what threatens him or her and the lives of innocent people. Someone who opposes injustice can do so empowered with a righteous indignation at the unjust suffering of others.

The virtues of courage and temperance are especially related to one another in that they regulate and direct our appetites or emotions. Temperance moderates our simple desiring (our "concupiscible" appetite, says

Aquinas) for goods like food, drink, and sex—and it moderates our sadness at not having them. Fortitude moderates our desire for what is difficult to attain or our tendency to flee what involves pain or discomfort (our "irascible" appetite). We see the interrelation of these two virtues in a particular way in the moderation of anger. Courage draws on a "righteous anger" to overcome a difficulty to attain a worthy good; but this anger must be moderated by the virtue of temperance to keep it in line with what is reasonable. We must use our good anger but master it, rather than be mastered by it.

Courage, like all of the virtues, requires prudence. As we saw in our discussion of prudence, a lack of proper forethought leads to imprudent decisions; and such imprudence is the source of recklessness which, as we will see, is contrary to the virtue of courage. Although it is temperance that moderates anger, it is prudence that determines what measure and expression of anger is reasonable in a particular situation. Courageous actions, empowered by a measured anger, must be guided by prudence.

Courage depends on the other virtues; and, at the same time, all of the other virtues require some measure of courage to the degree that they are confronted with challenges. To seek justice for others frequently requires the courage to face opposition. To grow in temperance, one must be able to confront challenges to one's effort to properly order one's desires. Prudent choices often cannot be made without fortitude. In fact, without the necessary courage to moderate undue fear, truly viable courses of action may be all too quickly dismissed because of their difficulty. In that case, the good to be obtained is undervalued relative to the obstacles to attain it; a lack of courage would thereby obscure the prudent choice.

The Vices Opposed to Fortitude

Vices arise, contrary to fortitude, either by defect or by excess. The absence or the lack of sufficient inner strength to reasonably confront obstacles and to overcome fear is the vice of cowardice or timidity. The abiding inclination to unreasonably deny the reality of threat is the vice of fearlessness. And closely related to the latter is the abiding tendency to confront obstacles or dangers that are too great, which is the vice of recklessness or foolhardiness.

Before we consider these contrary vices, we can also mention that, just as there are false or counterfeit forms of prudence, there are also acts that appear to flow from fortitude but do not. As we will see, the absence of reasonable fear may appear to be courageous, but this may be a false impression. One can lack fear because one is blind to or ignorant of the presence of real dangers. Such lack of knowledge can be innocent, or it could be a lack of prudent consideration, but the experience of fearlessness in such a situation might look like courage, but it is not. In a similar way, someone can confront dangers because of overwhelming passion or anger without thinking about danger. Again, this is not courage, but risky or daring action that is neither prudent nor temperate. There are, on the other hand, situations in which someone can possess skills or experience that can reasonably and safely allow them to confront situations that others would find dangerous. For example, it might be an act of real courage for a bystander to jump into the ocean to save a child who appears to be drowning. The same act by a trained and experienced lifeguard might not be an act of courage at all (though this is not to suggest that lifeguarding in general does not require courage).

Cowardice

Aquinas makes clear that fortitude is not fearlessness. As we have noted, fear in itself is a natural response to something that is perceived as a danger. We ought to fear what truly threatens us. Courage is not fearlessness. It is the refusal to give into fear, the ability to rise above fear in the face of a great good. A soldier going into battle, physicians about to treat people afflicted by life-threatening and infectious disease, and a patient facing the unknowns and possible complications of serious surgery ought to feel some amount of fear. The measure of courage is not the absence of reasonable fear, but rather the worthiness of the good and the ability to move forward despite the fear. Again, virtues bring "ease, smoothness, and promptitude," and fortitude allows us to confront danger and to experience reasonable fear with, at the same time, a kind of inner equilibrium that may not completely eliminate the fear, but will also not leave us paralyzed by it.

Courage, in fact, requires the recognition of one's vulnerability, the real possibility of being harmed. Soldiers in tanks do not normally require courage to face unarmed protesters. Bullies do not require courage to confront others who are smaller or weaker than they. It is the reality of real danger that makes for courage. Failing to recognize one's vulnerability, on the other hand, makes subsequent actions foolhardy, not courageous.

I once saw a television program about world-class professional cliff divers who dive off of platforms built on the edge of cliffs, some fifty-nine to eighty-five feet above the water. Their impact on hitting the water from that height would be sufficient, if not done properly, to kill a person instantly or to leave them severely injured and maimed. For virtually anyone else, this would be a very reckless behavior. But these elite divers have a great deal of experience and skill, and the sport takes whatever precautions are possible. Given the level of danger and the variability of wind and ocean, no amount of experience or skill would eliminate the need for courage to engage in this sport. One of the divers, however, commented that he always experiences some measure of fear each time that he dives. In fact, if he lost that fear entirely, he would have to leave the sport.

The vice of cowardice, then, is not simply the fact that someone experiences fear. To some degree, it is the presence of excessive fear—fear beyond what the actual danger or threat might warrant. But at its heart, cowardice is the inability to overcome fear. It is the inclination to be paralyzed by fear or the tendency not to rise to the challenge of confronting obstacles so that good can be accomplished. As we have seen, it can be a failure to embrace the good that is worthy of our effort.

When we think of courage, we naturally think immediately of the extraordinary or clearly heroic: martyrs and soldiers in battle. But there is, more often, a more ordinary kind of courage that must characterize every authentic human life. We must have the courage to confront the many challenges and struggles that arise in the ups-and-downs of our often ordinary lives. In the same way, when we think of cowardice, our minds might turn immediately to obvious and even extraordinary examples of cowardice in battle (though I suspect that those of us untested in the ugly realities of war would be reluctant to judge any soldier a coward). But again, cowardice can sadly be a more ordinary reality too. There is a kind of moral weakness that we can develop in ourselves that is unwilling or unable to rise to a challenge. It is possible to find ourselves unable to confront obstacles that need and deserve to be faced. There may be, of course, a variety of complex psychological reasons why some people cannot stand up for themselves, why some people seem unable to maintain the energy and focus to get a job done as it should be, or why other people seem immediately to shrink from confronting a problem and give in instead to dejection and depression. (There may, on the other hand, be psychological reasons why some people seem more naturally prone to fortitude.) But, at least when we look into our own hearts, amidst all of the complexity, we can sometimes see some amount of real moral fault—a failure to rise to a challenge that could have or should have been confronted.

Vices, like virtues, are built up over time, one choice after another. Whether we have some emotional propensity to fortitude or to its opposite, we become authentically courageous, one choice after another, one day after another. And we become cowardly—habitually unable to rise to challenges that we could reasonably hope to overcome—one choice after another. Hopefully we will never be confronted with a threat that would require truly heroic and extraordinary courage; but we will most certainly not be able to do so unless we can grow in a more ordinary fortitude. We must possess the virtue to confront threats that can arise suddenly and unexpectedly.

Again, the virtue of courage requires a desire for and a commitment to goodness. Cowardice, for its part, is a failure to adequately see and embrace such goodness. And sometimes we ourselves can be at fault for our failure to see, in front of us, goods that are truly worthy of our efforts. Unless we see the goodness and value of every human life, how could we rise to the courage to pursue justice, not only or even principally for ourselves, but for others? If we don't see the profound goodness of our own potential, our opportunities, our talents, and our God-given resources and friends, how can we rise to confront the challenges that are preventing us from being what we were meant to be? Unless we can be filled with wonder and gratitude at the gift of faith, how can we confront with courage the obstacles thrown up by our contemporary culture to the true living and growth in that faith?

Fearlessness

Fear, as we have seen, is a natural reaction to threat. Like other animals, we have an instinct for "fight or flight." The absence of such appropriate fear may be the result of some psychological problem or it may be some moral failing on our part. Just as someone who is experiencing despair or suicidal thoughts might lose a sense of the fundamental value of life for psychological reasons, it may be possible not to value one's own life sufficiently to experience fear of losing it. Or perhaps we might fail to value sufficiently other goods that are worthy of our pursuit, and so fail to fear their loss. Allowing ourselves to be overcome by sudden, uncontrollable anger or desire for vengeance might empower us to face great obstacles without fear, but such fearlessness is not an exercise of the virtue of courage, but rather a manifestation of the vice of intemperance.

Recklessness

A courageous choice must also be a prudent choice. Some dangers are too great to be met head-on. Sometimes retreat is the right response. The virtue of courage not only moderates fear, it also moderates the urge to be daring and engage in impulsive efforts to confront threats. In this sense, the vice of recklessness or foolhardiness is really a form of imprudence. There are thrill-seekers who understand the risks of what they do and take the necessary, available precautions. They might do what most of us would not—climb sheer cliffs or jump from planes for fun—but they are not necessarily reckless. There can also be people who seem at first glance to be truly brave but who are merely foolhardy. The imprudence of the foolhardy can take many forms: failure to ponder and weigh risks, negligence in taking adequate precautions, or carelessly (or with misplaced pride) overestimating one's abilities. We might think, for example, of drivers who are familiar with research that demonstrates that texting while driving is dangerous, but who somehow consider themselves immune to such risks. Such imprudence and its resulting recklessness may be accompanied by an absence of fear, but such fearlessness is again imprudent (and unjust to others who are put needlessly at risk), not courageous. It would be a very foolish form of pride to think oneself above the reality of fear, to overestimate one's abilities, or to underestimate real threats.

Virtues Related to Courage

Aquinas tells us that the virtue of courage has two modes: a posture of attack and a posture of endurance. Perhaps we most often think of courage in its attack mode: the soldier attacks the enemy; the firefighter, the flame; the person with cancer, the disease. But Aquinas tells us that the endurance mode of courage reveals its essence more clearly—not because enduring a difficulty is higher in itself, but because enduring over time manifests more clearly the sustained moral strength that is the essence of true courage. To endure when it is imprudent or impossible to attack reveals the true inner strength required of courage. Enduring is not necessarily passive. While there is no external action of attack, internally there is an inner strength that continues to work.

Magnanimity and magnificence are two virtues related to courage in its attacking mode. Perseverance and patience are two virtues related to courage in its enduring mode. Aquinas's discussion of these virtues offer us a great deal of insight to ponder.

Magnanimity

"Magnanimity" is not a frequently used term today, and we would probably not think of it as a virtue. It is rare to hear someone called "magnanimous." In its root, the word means "great-souled." So, a magnanimous person is someone with a largeness of spirit—a person with a big heart. In normal parlance, magnanimity can mean a general nobility of character. Or, in a more narrow sense, it signifies a person who is generous in forgiving or who quickly overlooks offenses or slights. It is the opposite, then, of petty, mean-spirited, or vindictive. These contemporary senses of the word "magnanimous" are consistent with what Aquinas means by the virtue of magnanimity, but his use is more narrowly focused on a virtue that is related to and promotes the virtue of courage.

Aquinas ties the virtue of magnanimity especially to the facing of difficulties to attain honor. This may at first seem odd, since it sounds like he is suggesting that it is a praiseworthy thing to face danger in order to attain worldly recognition and superficial forms of honor. But by honor, Aquinas is speaking more of a nobility of spirit, a fulfillment of what it means to be truly human, and the living of an authentic human life that gives bold testimony to others about how a human life ought to be lived. Magnanimous people, in Aquinas's sense of the word, are those who are inclined to confront even great difficulties to attain truly great goods—and, in their pursuit and attainment, to become the kind of men and women who genuinely fulfill what it means to be a fully alive human person. Magnanimity seeks the good not only for oneself, but for others—and honor, not in a superficial sense for self, but as an example of nobility of spirit for others.

We have seen that courage is always aimed at goodness, while cowardice is the inability to embrace goodness worthy of what is required to attain it. Courage, then, is strengthened by a clear-sighted vision of the good. The more clearly the worthiness of the goal is perceived, the more power we can find in ourselves to face what we must to attain it. The virtue of magnanimity is, in a way, the abiding inclination to "think big" or even to "dream big" about our goals. It is the abiding tendency to see the worthiness of a goal, to imagine the goodness of its attainment, and to see the reality of what separates us from the goal in relation to the higher value of its attainment. The magnanimous person is willing and able to undertake worthy but difficult tasks—to endure great hardships because he or she can sustain an image of what must be attained. Dr. Martin Luther King Jr., Mahatma Gandhi, and Saint Mother Teresa were magnanimous people.

Magnanimity is most obviously a virtue of dreamers who are able to realize great things. The building up of a large charitable organization from meager beginnings requires magnanimity. The people behind it must be able to keep before their own minds, in a sustained way, the worthiness of their enterprise and the dream of an organization that has the real potential of doing great things for those in need. Such people must be not only dreamers, but people with big dreams who also possess the strength and confidence to stay faithful to the struggle to make those big dreams a reality. We need politicians and leaders of every human community who can be truly magnanimous—who can rise to the challenges and needs of our time, but not for selfish gain or worldly honor. We need their efforts, and we need their example.

But magnanimity can also be far less heroic or seemingly extraordinary. The young single mother who imagines a better life for herself and her children and who finds the sustained strength to work and go to school is really a magnanimous person. She is a big-souled person who can keep a dream before her even as she confronts the challenges it requires, day after day, one after another. Or we can think of a young father confronted by cancer and the treatments necessary to cure it. It can take great courage to confront those obstacles and to fight the course of the disease. It is precisely this man's ability to keep before his mind's eye the image of his wife and children who love and need him that sustains his strength to fight on. This is courage, but it is a form of courage born of big dreams, worthy goals, and the resulting sustained strength to keep on fighting.

Magnanimity—as a greatness of soul—is not only about the ability to think big and sustain big effort. It is also a type of self-confidence in one's ability to attain one's goals. This is not pride. In fact, it's not really about self at all. It's about holding together the dream yet to be accomplished and a confidence in one's ability to realize it. Both are required for true magnanimity. This virtue includes a generosity with one's gifts as one pursues goods for one's own sake and for the sake of others. As people of faith, the element of self-confidence is grounded in a humble—and thus accurate and truthful—acknowledgement of our God-given abilities and our willingness to use them for good. Magnanimity brings with it, then, a kind of tranquility even in the face of great undertakings.

Again, we must recall that every virtue grows one choice at a time. One does not suddenly become courageous or magnanimous when confronted with a challenge or awakened to a dream. Sadly, it is possible to allow oneself to become someone who thinks small. Magnanimity is the opposite of the kind of pessimism, cynicism, a settling for less that can too easily afflict us. A history of disappointment or failure, of having shrunk from a good due to fear, or a lack of confidence can leave one with a sustained inability to see the real potential of attaining good, worthy, and even great things. Magnanimity then requires a kind of hope based on our own abilities, the assistance and support of others, and especially in what God can and will do. Without it, how would individuals ever become part of sustained efforts to bring real change to their own lives and to the world?

Vices Opposed to Magnanimity

It is a sign of the importance of magnanimity that Aquinas not only develops his reflection on it at some length, but that he also devotes time to its opposing vices. By excess, it is opposed by the vices of presumption, ambition, and vainglory. By defect, it is opposed by the vice of faintheartedness or timidity (traditionally called "pusillanimity").

Presumption is the vice of assuming that one is capable of what actually lies beyond one's capacities.[1] While magnanimity involves the capacity to think big with a healthy sense of self-confidence, it can also prudently assess the obstacles and its own limitations. The capacity to think big alone does not define magnanimity, but also the reasonable assessment of one's ability to harness one's skills, knowledge and God-given gifts to attain the desired good. The honor that the magnanimous person pursues—the nobility of spirit which characterizes the person willing to seek out worthy goals—also requires the humility of recognizing the limits of our still frail

---

1. Aquinas also discusses a different kind of presumption in relation to the theological virtue of hope (*ST* II-II, q. 21). In that context, presumption is a kind of false hope in God's mercy and goodness—for example, simply expecting God's gift of eternal life without our repentance and ongoing conversion in this life.

humanity. Presumption is the vice of thinking big without the reasonable assessment of the actual limitations of one's abilities to realize one's dreams.

In contemporary terms, the word "*ambition*" can have a positive sense of possessing the energy and drive to get things done and to succeed in one's endeavors. A young person, fresh out of college and starting a promising new job, needs the positive drive that can be called ambition. At the same time, the word "ambition" may also have a negative connotation. For Aquinas, ambition is the desire for honor gone amuck. It seeks a superficial and worldly honor as an end—which is the opposite of the true honor of a magnanimous person. Rather than seeking a great good by confronting great difficulty and thereby attaining the nobility of spirit that others can rightly admire and aspire to imitate, ambition seeks honor for its own sake. As we have seen, there is no virtue when the end sought is evil. And worldly honor is no worthy end in itself. Magnanimity always involves using one's gifts and abilities to attain goodness in a good way for good motives in regard to others.

Vainglory, as its name suggests, is the pursuit of a vain or superficial glory in the eyes of others. It seeks praise for what is not worthy of praise, seeks it from people who are not in a position to offer valid praise, or seeks it without reference to God, from whom all goodness flows and who empowers every good action. Magnanimity has nothing to do with human praise or superficial glory for its own sake—and certainly not as an end to be sought. The magnanimous person seeks what is truly good, acknowledging that its accomplishment is not simply his or her doing. In the end, vainglory is related to pride.

Aquinas offers one brief but very interesting article to the "offspring" of vainglory. This vice results in boasting in words, the desire to be seen as possessing the latest or the very newest, or putting on a false show of one's pretended gifts or possessions ("hypocrisy"). Since the vainglorious person does not want to appear inferior to another, the vice may result in obstinacy, holding stubbornly to one's own opinion or viewpoint. This is often coupled with an unwillingness to give up one's perspectives, plans, and priorities in collaboration with others (which Aquinas calls "discord"). Vainglory may lead a person to be contentious with others—defending one's viewpoint in a manner that draws attention to the vainglorious person's need to be right. The final offspring of vainglory is an unwillingness to be subordinate to the direction or supervision of others. In light of our reflection in the previous chapter, we can see that vainglory's "offspring" are also often forms of injustice.

Presumption, ambition, and vainglory may mask themselves in action as the virtue of magnanimity, but they are misdirected and excessive in their pursuit of the mere appearance of true honor for self. Faintheartedness (or timidity), on the other hand, is the failure to rise to the pursuit of worthy goals, even though one possesses the ability to overcome the obstacles that stand in the way. The fainthearted or timid person is "small-spirited" and/ or lacks both the self-confidence commensurate with his or her actual gifts, as well as the willingness to envision or embrace worthy goals. The quintessential Gospel example is the servant whose master gave him an amount of money with which to make a profit, but who instead buried it in the ground where it did nothing for anyone (Matt 25:14–30; Luke 19:11–27). This may have the appearance of humility, but true humility sees the truth of one's abilities, neither overestimating them (presumption) nor underestimating them (faintheartedness).

Perhaps even more than the other vices opposed to magnanimity, it is faintheartedness that is the greatest threat to the society around us, whether that society is our nation or culture, or whether it is the society of the family. Faintheartedness (or timidity) is a failure of the person to embrace his or her own gifts. It is a failure to envision and embrace what is truly good. It is a lack of resolve to accomplish the good. Therefore, it is a diminishment of the person. The timid person refuses to rise to what he or she can be and accomplish. This has sad consequences for the world around them. Some great good is left undone. Faintheartedness is passed on to others who might also have the necessary ability, but who are influenced by others whose example they might have reason to respect. They are "dis-couraged." The collaboration that might arise among those who, together, could accomplish the good is left behind.

We live in a world in great need of good action, positive example, and authentic witness to what it means to be truly human in relationship with others. If we are fainthearted in the use of our strength and skills to overcome injustice and seek peace, to do the right and defend the good, to live and promote the faith, we will diminish ourselves as persons, give sad and sickly example to others, and let evil and indifference have their way.

The Virtue of Magnificence

Aquinas tells us that there is a specific virtue for those who pursue great works—and have the capacity to accomplish them. The word "magnificence" today usually means grand, lavish, splendid, or perhaps garish and showy. But for Aquinas, it is the virtue by which people with ample financial means seek to do great things for their communities or for God. It is, then, the great philanthropist's virtue. It allows someone to part with a portion of their wealth with relative ease in order to accomplish something that will truly benefit others. Magnificence thereby overcomes excessive reluctance or anxiety about making a donation which a person of means can, in fact, afford. It is this sustained ability to face the obstacle of giving or spending that is its relation to the virtue of fortitude. Magnificence overcomes the inner obstacles that true and significant generosity can require. There are people with great wealth who live in unreasonable fear that some calamity will arise and they will no longer be able to live as they have. It is magnificence that would allow such people to regulate their fear in light of prudent risks in order to contribute generously to a truly worthy enterprise.

The distribution of wealth in society raises larger questions of justice—principles of justice, just economic structures, and the virtue of justice. Without denying the importance of issues of justice, the virtue of magnificence focuses on the character of the person who is blessed with great possessions. And the fact is, in our affluent society, that there are many people with great wealth and thus with the potential to help society and its members in significant ways. What constitutes wealth, of course, is relative. But Aquinas's reflection on the virtue of magnificence should give people of means pause to think of what they might be able to accomplish for the good of others with a generous—"magnificent"—sharing of their resources.

The fact is that our affluent society also perpetuates consumerism and materialism. It is easy enough for those with material wealth to focus its use on themselves and what their money can buy for themselves: cars, homes, vacations, gadgets, bling. Tax benefits for charitable giving can be a good incentive for the wealthy to give. And that's a good thing. But it doesn't necessarily constitute the virtue of magnificence, which is not simply a matter of practical benefits for charitable giving, but an inner, abiding tendency to share what they have to accomplish good things with their resources. It requires, then, a freedom from simple self-seeking. An affluent society needs the virtue of magnificence more than ever.

In the history of the Catholic Church in the United States, the building of its parish and school buildings depended on the hard work and generous donations of ordinary, working-class people. Visiting grand old churches in old city neighborhoods gives witness to what the generosity of many people coming together can accomplish. And yet, many Catholic institutions such as hospitals, colleges, seminaries, and other schools—and more recently, their endowments—have also depended on the large donations of people with both great faith and great resources. The growth and maintenance of such institutions has required the magnanimity of many Catholic donors. Today, it seems that the younger generations are no longer so inclined to support institutions in general and the institutional church in particular. Surely there are many reasons for such a shift, but it is to be lamented to the degree that it is a failure of faith, institutional commitment to the church, and/or the virtue of magnificence.

Magnificence encourages generous giving, but it also moderates it. As a virtue, it seeks the true good, not garish display or self-serving recognition, as its name might seem to imply. It is not foolish or wasteful. Again, magnificence must be guided by prudence. Like magnanimity, it promotes virtue in others through good example. The wealthy who are truly generous—magnificent, in this sense—can be an example and incentive to their financial peers. The community projects pursued by the magnificent can encourage others to rise to the challenge.

The contrary of the virtue of magnificence is meanness or littleness. It is the vice of those who possess great resources but refuse to put them to work for the good of others. They have great wealth, but small goals for the benefit of others. Or they can see the great good that their wealth could accomplish, but they cannot bring themselves to expend what it would take, even though it is prudently within their means. Or, having set out to finance a truly noble project, they then pull back and begin to unnecessarily pinch pennies and thereby prevent the undertaking from becoming what it might have.

Patience

As we have said, for Aquinas, the virtue of fortitude has both an attacking and an enduring mode. The virtues of patience and perseverance are related to its enduring mode. Because undergoing difficulty over time can require the greater strength, these virtues of endurance can often give greater evidence of the true meaning of courage. There are certainly situations and periods in our lives that require these enduring virtues—the sustained ability to hold on, which is not the same as passive resignation or giving up. The people who can endure in the face of hardship, struggle, sickness, and tragedy can truly be among the most courageous.

Patience is the virtue that allows a person to withstand suffering or difficulty without giving into despair, unjustified anger, or overpowering sadness. It is the ability to maintain an inner tranquility of spirit in the face of challenging circumstances. It is not the same thing as an attitude of passivity. Some situations demand action. It is not patience to refuse to act when a good is at stake and one has the power to overcome the evil that threatens it. As always, it is prudence that helps to determine when endurance or attack is the most appropriate response.

Some people may have a natural tendency to the virtue of patience. These people possess a more laid-back attitude, a great natural ability to "roll with the punches," as we say. It may be less of a challenge for them to be patient in the face of life's challenges, both great and small. On the other hand, such people may find themselves too easily passive in the face of challenges that really ought to be confronted. Being laid back is not always the best attitude, just as patient endurance must sometimes give way to courageous attack.

People in every age have had to develop the virtue of patience to face life's inconveniences and challenges. But perhaps it is true that, in our age, patience is a more difficult virtue to form and maintain. We live in a world of instant gratification. We have so many conveniences and devices that have reduced our need to wait. The Internet allows us to gain information almost instantaneously and to order whatever products we might want without leaving our homes (with expedited shipping, if desired). We no longer need to wait for the exchange of paper letters. Today, when we send an email or a text message, we can reasonably expect a quick response—in fact, we may find ourselves irritated if the recipient of our message fails to respond upon receipt. We seem in constant pursuit of better ways to avoid the need to grow in patience.

The virtue of patience is an interior, abiding attitude that provides an inner peace while waiting in line or in traffic, while nearby young parents struggle to quiet their overactive young kids, or until the "next available representative" can handle our call. Certainly, there are situations in which there is no good reason why we should be made to wait, but there are many others in which patience is really the only appropriate response. Patient people know how to maintain their inner calm while waiting, who can confront the challenge that must simply be endured for a time, and who possesses the inner nobility of spirit to carry themselves with due composure as a witness to those around them.

Surely we have all witnessed the person who goes into a rage at the airline ticket agent who is simply trying to reroute one passenger after another when a flight has been canceled or delayed by weather. We have seen the person who starts ranting and raving in a checkout line because an elderly person is taking time to find their wallet or slowly and carefully write out a check. Perhaps we have faced the frustration of a fellow driver who apparently thinks that we are driving too slowly through congested traffic. In fact, maybe, at one time or another, we ourselves have been one or the other of those impatient people. Patience is the virtue that keeps us from being "that" person. It is the virtue that gives us the inner sense that such impatience in the face of such trivial inconveniences is not really fitting to the person that we want to be.

But patience shows its true nobility in the face of greater trials. Illness that cannot be cured or suffering that cannot be alleviated demand a deeper patience. Caring for elderly parents who suffer from dementia or Alzheimer's disease requires a profound patience. The innocent Jesus, confronted with his undeserved suffering, is a model of patience for those who must endure what cannot be changed. But patience in the face of life's sometimes great challenges is built up by a patient response to the countless little inconveniences of daily life.

Perseverance

Perseverance, like patience, is a virtue of endurance, but it is more directly related to a goal actively being sought. The good that patience seeks is the tranquility and nobility of spirit that cannot be trampled by hardship; for its part, perseverance prevents giving up on a worthy goal, although its attainment remains at a distance and obstacles remain to be confronted. Perseverance, like all virtues, is directed to the moral good of the person who possesses it, but it is more directly related to an exterior good. The virtue of perseverance is the abiding tendency and ability to persist in the pursuit of good despite delays, the need for prolonged effort, and the multiplication of obstacles. Perseverance resists discouragement and the temptation to give up on a goal which has been perceived and embraced as truly worthy. It reveals the true power of the human spirit to endure. The development of real athletic skill in order to excel at competitive sports, the pursuit of serious scholarship, or getting a college degree while holding down part-time jobs and caring for a family—all of these require perseverance.

Aquinas distinguishes perseverance from constancy, though the difference is a nuance. The former is the persistence that keeps us on course in the face of hardships that arise immediately in the pursuit of a goal. The latter is the persistence that allows us to continue despite obstacles that are external to the effort itself. An older college student is "persevering" in staying the course with his or her studies despite the difficulties and effort that academic goals require (that is, these difficulties arise from the pursuit of the good itself). On the other hand, that same student is "constant" in the face of other problems such as illness, financial setbacks, or the encroachment of other responsibilities that may arise (that is, these are difficulties that are not part of the attainment of the good itself but arise from outside it). Perhaps for our purposes, it is easiest to include both under the titles of perseverance.

Of course, sometimes situations reveal that even our prudent decision to begin could not have foreseen the actual difficulties to be confronted. In such cases, prudence might demand giving up or at least rethinking our realistic hopes and our strategies. Fighting a disease like cancer, for example, can require great fortitude in facing the treatments and their side effects—and simply in the refusal to be paralyzed by fear. It can demand great patience as one waits to see the effectiveness of treatments, the results of tests, and the considered recommendations of physicians as they ponder the next step in a line of treatment. Battling serious disease can require perseverance through multiple treatments and their side effects. Such courage, patience, and perseverance can be truly praiseworthy and reveal the nobility of character of the person who struggles on. It can manifest their love for life and for family, their faith, and their clear-sighted perception of the good. At the same time, each step in such a struggle demands the prudence to reevaluate, rethink, and make new decisions. A point may come at which it becomes clear that perseverance in the fight is no longer the best path. Persistence in faith and patience in the midst of dying becomes instead the most appropriate attitude.

The effort to grow in any virtue often requires perseverance. One must be persistent in the face of temptations to be unchaste, impatient, or imprudent. Living the Christian life itself requires such constancy. Although the perseverance specifically to grow in the Christian life and in the life of prayer requires the infused form of perseverance which comes with grace, this does not deny the importance of perseverance as a natural virtue in every aspect of our lives. One of my brother monks likes to say that being Christian is easy—the hard part is doing it one day after the other. As we likely all know from experience, the effort to grow in the spiritual life and specifically in the life of prayer also requires perseverance, given in grace and acquired by our effort. Steady perseverance in prayer and the development of a true habit of prayer that can remain through inevitable periods of dryness requires great persistence. This is a point made especially by Saint Teresa of Avila, one of the greatest teachers of prayer in the Christian tradition. She insisted that we must begin and continue the life of prayer with a "very determined determination" (una muy determinada determinación). We must never give up on prayer, no matter what happens or how often we might fail or fall into sin. Anyone who has tried to grow in prayer knows how profoundly true this is.

The opposite of perseverance is the vice which we might translate as moral weakness, feebleness, or irresoluteness. It is the vice of those who are unable to remain resolute and determined in the face of difficulties that are not objectively insurmountable in order to attain a worthy good. Perhaps we have all found ourselves unable to rise to the maintenance of our New Year's resolutions—to stay on a diet, to maintain our fitness regimen, or to persevere in daily prayer. These failures may be the result of starting with an overly idealistic or hazy goal, a lack of real resolve in the beginning, or the absence of workable strategies to get where we want to go. But it is important to see that it is possible to possess a real vice or irresoluteness that makes it difficult for us to rise to virtually any serious challenge. It is one thing to fail on a diet from time to time (or even completely) if the goal is mostly a matter of appearance rather than averting a real health threat. It is quite another to possess an abiding moral weakness that keeps us from staying on course. Growth in all of the moral virtues, in faithful Christian discipleship, and in prayer are just a few examples of important matters that require an ability to stick with a plan.

Perseverance, like all of the natural virtues, grows over time, one decision after another. And perseverance in one area of our life can empower us in others. Aquinas would certainly say that we do not fully or perfectly possess the virtue of perseverance unless and until it empowers us in every area of our life. Still, we can find ourselves persistent in one area but not another. A young person might be determined in pursuing athletic prowess with all of the training that it requires, but remain quite irresolute when it comes to consistently putting the necessary effort into academic studies. We are all capable of such compartmentalizing, but sometimes if we can grow more persistent in one area, it can carry over into others.

The virtue of perseverance also has a counterfeit. There are people who are simply stubborn and obstinate, or who just refuse to seem to fail in what they have resolved to do. Such resolution is at best a false perseverance. It fails in pursuit of a true good—that is, it seeks to "be right" or to appear undefeated. Authentic virtue is not about self-serving goals, and it is always guided by prudence that knows when holding on no longer makes sense. Perseverance is not stubbornness or obstinacy.

The virtue of courage is more necessary for good daily living than we might commonly think. It may be that we need it more than we usually think, or it may be that we possess it in forms that we ourselves would not have thought of as instances of courage. Hopefully, we will not need an attacking mode of courage in the face of extraordinary danger or difficulty. Hopefully, we will never face the threat of physical attack, the need to run into a burning building or jump into a river to save a child, or the reality of persecution or martyrdom for the Christian faith (which is, sadly, still a present reality in the contemporary world). But we won't be able to muster such extraordinary courage without the daily, ordinary efforts to confront and to endure life's inevitable little challenges, unless we can "stay the course" in the midst of life's choppy waters and sudden storms, unless we can be both big-souled and, at the same time, persevere and remain patient.

5

Temperance

(*ST* II-II, qq. 141–70)

BALANCE, MODERATION, AND INNER harmony: these are words that we all wish would describe our daily lives. But in today's busy world, for many of us, they often do not. Life around us can be hectic and demanding. We can find ourselves pulled in many different directions at once, trying to juggle a variety of balls at one time—job, family, elderly parents, volunteer responsibilities, adequate rest, healthy eating, regular exercise, and prayer.

Sometimes the external chaos matches an internal sense of disorder. Various good things and desires tug at our attention and energy at the same time. We love our families and want to spend time with them. We feel responsibility for our elderly parents. We are ambitious in our work, perhaps in good and bad ways. We like the finer things that more income could provide for ourselves and others, even at the cost of more hours of work. We know we should eat better, but the fast food is convenient and oh-so-tasty. More regular exercise would probably benefit us in many ways, but it's hard to make it—or prayer and good reading—a priority.

Imbalance, immoderation, and the lack of harmony can be both external and internal. Exterior things can create a sense of chaos around us, even while our interior desires and sense of responsibility can swirl around within us. Even more deeply, there are appetites that can seem to get the best of us, sometimes drawing close to the level of addictions: our appetites for food, drink, and sexual pleasure. An abiding anger can take hold within us, leading us to say and do things that we know are not helpful to anyone, including ourselves. A desire to "get ahead," the need to be held in high regard and even envied by others, and the appetite for more of life's glitter and glitz can come to consume us.

If we are lucky, there are times when it seems that "the stars have aligned," and the external disorder clears for a time. But the truth is, as experience has probably taught us all, whatever the situation around us, a real sense of harmony must come from within. Usually an external balance and order must flow from an internal balancing and ordering. This is more than just a matter of good time management (though it is not unrelated to it). Guided by the virtue of prudence, we must learn to order our priorities at this moment in our lives with the resources that are reasonably available to us: job, family, volunteer efforts, and healthy self-care. More deeply, we must order and balance our inner desires in keeping with what is really healthy and good for ourselves and those for whom we are responsible. This is the concern of the virtue of temperance.

Disordered Selves in a Disordered World

At various times in its history, Christianity might justly have been accused of being suspicious of human desire itself, especially our inclination to satisfy our bodily wants: food, drink, and sex. And if our yearnings were seen as suspect, so too the pleasure that would accompany the satisfying of our desires. There was a time in the church, at least among some prominent teachers, when sex and its accompanying pleasure was suspect even in marriage. In such a context, the virtue of temperance might take on the appearance of the ability to suppress, deny, or overcome one's natural desires. But this is not the vision of Saint Thomas Aquinas about human desires, nor about the virtue of temperance.

For Aquinas, our basic human desires are good. God created us with desires for food, for drink, and for sex because these things are necessary for our personal survival and for the continuance of the human race. The things that we naturally desire—and our desires for them—are good in themselves. Furthermore, the pleasure in attaining them is good, encouraging us to seek what we, in fact, need for ourselves and for the human race. For Aquinas, pleasure in itself is not suspect. Our desires were given to us to help us to seek and attain what is truly good for and worthy of human persons.

But, of course, things are not exactly as God created them to be. Sin is a reality in the world around and within each of us. And sin has distorted our desiring so that we desire things in inappropriate measure, in unsuitable ways or circumstances, or in conflict with higher or more urgent goods to be sought. In this context, pleasure comes to be, not the accompaniment and reward of attaining a good in appropriate measure and circumstances, but an end in itself. Or pleasure becomes the reward of some action that itself is not appropriate to the time, place, or person. In the end, we can easily experience ourselves as disordered in our desires—a lack of proper order to which we can be blind or which, once seen, can be very difficult to make right.

Added to our inner lack of moderation and balance—and contributing to it—are the enticements of a world of sin. There are certainly examples and messages in the world that encourage us toward the good, but there is no lack of negative messages and lures as well. Advertising—reflecting the values prevailing in society—entices us to eat foods that are unhealthy. Super-sized meals and all-you-can-eat buffets encourage us to eat far more than we need. Heavy consumption of alcohol is a problem on college campuses, and many people find that they can hardly attend a social function in which alcohol is not a prominent feature. Our society and its entertainment media is saturated with enticements to free sexual satisfaction. Certainly, there is actual pornography, cheap and readily available via the Internet, but even prime time television in its programming and commercials has no lack of strong sexual messages and enticements.

What the Virtue of Temperance Is

For Thomas Aquinas, temperance is the virtue that disposes us to proper balance, moderation, and due measure in realizing our desires, especially our bodily desires for food, drink, and sex (i.e., related especially, he says, to the sense of touch). He tells us that, because these goods are so fundamental and necessary for human existence, we can experience our desire for them even more intensely than our desire for higher goods like truth and beauty. Like all of the virtues, temperance directs us to a life worthy of a mature human person, pursuing what is authentically good for us in properly human ways. Temperance is not directed to denying, suppressing, or repressing our desires, but to moderating them so that they truly lead us to what is good for us and for others in the circumstances in which we find ourselves. Temperance is not the enemy of pleasure, but rather the disposition to find pleasure in the right action at the right time in pursuit of the truly good.

"Self-mastery" is a term that is often used to define temperance. Temperate persons are the "masters" of themselves in the sense of being able to order or even control their desires. Perhaps words like "mastery" and "control" might continue to imply a level of suspicion about desire in itself; but, at the same time, anyone who has tried to order an unbalanced desire for food, drink, or sexual satisfaction knows that the effort can very much feel like trying to master or control that desire. Virtues, as we have seen, lend "ease, smoothness, and promptitude" in seeking the good. The truly temperate person, for example, does not experience a constant struggle in resisting the urge to eat in an unhealthy manner or amount. But, short of its attainment, growth in this virtue is not really inaccurately described by such words, as our own experience would undoubtedly attest.

The virtue of temperance is based on a vision, or at least a sense of what it means to be authentically human, with one's desires and choices in line with what we know to be truly good for us. It includes the desire and self-possession to live in accord with what is truly worthy of a good human life. In this sense, temperance is a kind of moral integrity, a convergence of our wants and choices with our true good, together with the ability to live consistently in this integrity.

Without temperance, we cannot fully accomplish other goods by making appropriate responses. The intemperate person, ruled by disordered wants, can be hindered from seeing and choosing rightly. An immoderate desire for food, drink, or sexual satisfaction can cloud one's sense of how to prudently act in regard to the priorities that guide one's decisions, how to justly relate and interact with other persons, and one's ability to rise to face the obstacles that stand in the way of realizing the good.

Like all of the virtues, temperance is guided by prudence. It is not possible to have an absolute rule for what or how much people should eat or drink. People's caloric needs vary according to gender, body size, levels of physical activity, and the like. While restraint may be the temperate response in one situation, special celebrations may call for a different but still temperate balance. What constitutes temperate and chaste sexual desire and activity varies according to one's state in life and to the immediate circumstances and people involved. The balance and moderation that temperance brings is not a one-size-fits-all measure. Truly temperate people are also necessarily prudent people who can discern the appropriate responses at different times and in a variety of situations.

Interestingly, Aquinas reminds us that we have not only positive desires that move us to seek pleasant things, but also desires to avoid what is disagreeable to us. But sometimes unpleasant things cannot or should not be avoided. The temperate person can eat something simply because it is healthy, even if it is not as desirable as something less healthy—choose the healthy options on a salad bar rather than the unhealthy but desirable. He or she can drink the medicine that carries a horrible aftertaste, because it is important. The person who possesses temperance is ruled neither by desires to obtain the pleasant, nor by desires always to shun the unpleasant.

In a similar way, Aquinas tells us that temperance not only moderates our desires. It also orders our disappointment or sorrow when we are denied what we want. Young children want what they want, when they want it. When they fail to get the food that they want or are presented with what they do not want, they cannot control their disappointment. Often enough, they simply start to cry, or even throw a tantrum. No normal adult would do the same, but the same feeling can easily arise. The decision to eat healthier or to fast—and thus to deny oneself the food that one wants—can be difficult; but we can react to this denial in a variety of ways. Dieting can put some people out of sorts, just as fasting can make others look glum, somber, or sad (Matt 6:16). Temperance moderates both our desiring and our disappointment in not possessing.

Elements of Temperance

Aquinas identifies two elements or components of temperance which are not virtues in themselves. They are difficult to understand and to translate into contemporary English. In Latin, they are *verecundia* (q. 144), which is traditionally translated as shame or shamefacedness, and *honestas* (q. 145), which is translated as honesty, or perhaps more loosely as a sense of honor.

Saint Thomas speaks of *verecundia* as the desire not to appear "base." He tells us that, like other animals, we naturally desire food, drink, and sex. But we are not just any kind of animal. We are human persons, created in the image of God, with the ability to moderate our desire in light of what is good and appropriate to us and our circumstances. To be controlled by our appetites, then, he tells us, makes us like simple animals—that is, "base." In more contemporary terms, we could say that *verecundia* is the disposition not to be—nor appear to be—immoderate, unbalanced, or driven by our appetites. In other words, it keeps us from offering a bad example of the authentic integrity proper to human beings that comes with moderation and balance.

The traditional English translation of *verecundia* is the word "shame," which has virtually no positive connotations in contemporary usage. "Being shamed" or "shaming others" for their appearance, for example, is rightly seen as seriously wrong. We see that it is unhealthy for people to carry a sense of shame for events or situations from the past. But, for Aquinas, *verecundia* is not about shame in this contemporary sense. It is quite the opposite, in fact. He is suggesting that the virtue of temperance rests on a sense of self-respect and pride in oneself so that one would not want to be ruled by one's desires—or be perceived by others in that way. Aquinas is conscious of the fact that we live in community, in relation with others. Our individual virtues are not only our personal excellences, but fit into and promote a virtuous society. *Verecundia* is the healthy sense of one's own true worth as a human person and the desire not to act in such a way as to mar that authentic vision of a well-ordered life for self or others.

Most probably, in light of contemporary usage, it would be impossible to use the word "shame" as an adequate translation for Aquinas's *verecundia*. At the same time, it can be noted that we can speak of healthy guilt and unhealthy guilt, authentic guilt and inauthentic guilt. While it is true that we don't want to feel or encourage guilt where there is no wrong or no responsibility, we can speak of a good guilt that we should feel when we have done wrong. Authentic guilt is a result of a healthy moral sense of right and wrong. It moves us to change and move forward. In the same way, without trying to argue for the reclamation of the word "shame" as such, I think Aquinas's teaching here distinguishes an unhealthy sense of shame from the disquiet that we should feel within ourselves when our disordered desires have gotten the better of us. Perhaps the prudish-sounding question "Have you no shame?" might be better stated as "Have you no sense of pride or respect in yourself as a person of moral integrity?"

I recall, many decades ago, reading a text on Catholic sexual ethics that included a section on a "healthy sense of shame." Even then, it seemed to me an unfortunate phrase, although I understood that the author was suggesting that couples should have enough respect for their bodies and sexuality, and especially for the intimacy of their physical sharing, not to parade it around in public in crass ways. Now, what constitutes inappropriate or immodest behavior varies in cultures and situations, but I came to a better understanding of the concept while a passenger on a plane. Dressed in priestly attire, I was seated next to young couple who could hardly keep their hands off each other for the entirety of the flight (to the point that their behavior would have made for a PG rating if it were on the big screen). It made for an awkward flight. But it made me recall the need for that (unfortunately titled) "healthy sense of shame"—not that what the couple was doing was necessarily morally wrong in itself, but it seemed to me that they were cheapening what should have been an intimate physical expression of their love for one another by putting it on display for those around them. They should have had a better sense of themselves as persons and of the intimate beauty of their sexual sharing.

The other element of temperance, according to Aquinas, is what he calls *honestas*. It appears to be the equivalent of the English word "honesty." But for Aquinas, in this context, it is not about truth-telling. If one looks up the etymology of the English word "honesty," one finds that its original meaning, now obsolete, is honor, decency, or uprightness. An "honest" person in that older sense is an upright person, and this is closer to the meaning of Aquinas's *honestas*.

As an essential component of temperance, *honestas* is the ability to appreciate moral beauty, and especially the beauty of the person whose desires are well-ordered to goodness and to what is truly worthy of the person. It is therefore the ability to desire it and appreciate it within oneself. When we admire physical beauty, we are appreciating the ordered features and proportion of a person or thing. When we admire moral beauty, we are appreciating good order and proportion in judging reality and its demands, ordered desires that lead to good action, and actions that are in proportion to the real demands of the situation. If we hope to be physically healthy and fit, we must value and desire the beauty of health and fitness. If we hope to be morally good and, in this case, temperate, we must appreciate the beauty and dignity of a well-ordered interior life.

By speaking of *verecundia* and *honestas* as the necessary elements of the virtue of temperance. Aquinas is telling us that the ability to moderate and order our desires to what is really good depends on a sense of oneself in relation to others. To arrive at being temperate, we must be able to see ourselves as possessing a dignity, as authentic human persons, that is worthy of pursuing and maintaining. Temperance is not simply a narrow focus on right desires but, more broadly, on how our desires and the choices that follow from them impact who we are in the context of community. The moral disorder of others impacts us constantly—as our disorder would impact others. How can the people around us grow in a sense of what it means to be authentically human and to act in authentically human ways if we do not have an appreciation of or give witness to such authenticity in our own living?

Vices Opposed to Temperance

If temperance is moderation and balance in desiring, its opposing vices involve immoderation and imbalance. This can take two forms: an excessive control of desire or, more commonly, a lack of rational control over our appetites for our authentic good.

Intemperance as Insensitivity to Desire and Pleasure

We might immediately think of anything that goes by the name of intemperance as a kind of excess of desire, but Aquinas introduces his discussion of intemperance by reflecting on a type of exaggerated ordering of desire and a refusal of ordinary and appropriate human pleasure which is called *insensitivity*. As we have seen, Aquinas has a positive view of human desire in itself and of the pleasure that accompanies the enjoyment of the good. And it is precisely because desire and pleasure are essentially human that their inordinate repression is wrong.

In our day, in which inordinate desire is more probably the far greater reality, it may be hard to imagine a vice, for example, of too little desire for or pleasure in sex in marriage or too little eating. In fact, when such things are the reality today, we rightly think immediately of some emotional, relational, or psychological foundation rather than about immorality or vice. Aquinas recognizes that insensitivity to desire and pleasure, in moral terms, is not the more usual form of intemperance. And, in this context, he is not speaking about a kind of emotional or psychological incapacity to feel, but an excess of control or active repression of what is authentically human. Perhaps today, in the form of the vice of intemperance, it would take the form, for example, not of anorexia or bulimia, but of the person who goes overboard in dieting or other forms of unhealthy eating. In our day, even short of real psychological issues, there are people who are so obsessed with their health that they become virtually unable to have a good meal or a drink, even in special circumstances with special people.

Nor, by speaking of intemperance in the form of insensitivity, is Aquinas denying the positive value of fasting, abstinence, or other forms of asceticism in the spiritual life. In fact, he addresses these practices even before he begins to speak of insensitivity. But such traditional spiritual means are guided by the infused virtue of temperance, which sees the authentic good of the human person in the broader perspective, not only of physical health, but also in relation to one's transcendent end in union with God.

The Vice of Intemperance

More typical are forms of intemperance by excess involving a failure to properly order desire according to what is truly right and good for the person. Again, to speak of intemperance in our contemporary world requires us to distinguish between a real moral vice, which is a matter of our bad choices over time and emotional or psychological compulsions. More specifically, we must distinguish between the vice of intemperance and various forms of addictions—of which Thomas Aquinas could not have been aware in his day. It is true that the vice of intemperance can easily become a matter of addiction. And while addiction may not remove all moral responsibility, it moves the matter of desire and choice beyond primarily moral categories. In the same way, what constitutes intemperate behaviors can vary according to times, cultures, persons, and circumstances—for example, what constitutes drinking to excess—but neither the recognition of the reality of addiction nor the acceptance of relevant cultural differences negates Aquinas's valuable insights into desires that are not ordered to what is authentically human and good for self and others.

The vice of intemperance, simply put, is the opposite of temperance. It involves the habitual disposition to disordered desire, to the pursuit of pleasure for its own sake apart from any other good, to immoderate choices and to imbalance in choosing. Just as a virtue brings "ease, smoothness, and promptness" in doing the good, intemperance brings ease in falling prey to one's desires, even when the result will not be good for self or others. Intemperate people are "slaves" of their own desiring and cravings. Again, the problem is neither desire nor pleasure in themselves. But desire should direct us to what is truly good for us and for others, and authentic pleasure is meant to be the reward of the good attained. For the intemperate person, desire is out of whack, and inner imbalance and lack of harmony is easily reflected in an outer imbalance and disharmony.

Aquinas follows Aristotle in calling intemperance a "childish" vice, because it is like an unruly and out of control child: unreasonable, undisciplined, willful, wants its own way, unable to stop, and grows more unruly when it is indulged. And, like a child, it can only be set on the right path by curbing and restraining its desires. But Aquinas has even stronger words about intemperance. He says that it lowers human beings to the level of animals who are not guided by reason and conscious direction to the good, but by bodily instinct. In doing so, he is not denigrating the fact that human beings are, in fact, animals; but intemperance goes contrary to what is truly and distinctively human, which is our ability to choose what is good for us. For good or for ill, other animals most generally simply follow their instincts. There is no true moral praise or blame in that case. But human beings can decide to act for or against their inclinations to what is good, and to decide wrongly over time leaves us with an acquired tendency to act in a disordered way.

Intemperance is a vice that impacts our deciding and acting more generally. In fact, it can impact even our view of the world around us. When our desires betray us—when they pull us to what is not truly good for us and for others—it impacts our decision-making more generally. In life, there are many circumstances in which we must decide what is truly good over and above what might be the most desirable and pleasurable at this moment. Intemperance disrupts our ability to choose rightly, even when we can see the greater or immediate good at stake. But more, inordinate desire can skew our vision, focusing our attention on what we desire and making us blind to what is truly good. In more traditional terms, intemperance dims the intellect and weakens the will.

Kinds of Temperance

Aquinas identifies virtues that are really forms of temperance in the different realms of our desiring: temperance in eating, in drinking, and in sex.

Temperance in Eating

Aquinas notes, without much comment, that it is possible to be intemperate in eating by eating too little—that is, by suppressing or ignoring the desire to eat and to enjoy the pleasure of eating in moderation when it is appropriate and healthy. The natural desire to eat is meant to lead us to do what is essential for our life and health. One is intemperate in eating, then, when one follows faddish diets that are overly restrictive of food in a way that is not healthy (for example, in trying to lose weight too quickly). Again, we are not talking about actual eating disorders.

Aquinas calls the virtue of temperance in eating—the habitual disposition to eat the right foods, at the appropriate time, in the right amount—*abstinence*. He notes that the word can also be used in other contexts to refer to moderation in drinking, or really the sustained ability to refrain from anything. We might also think of the religious practice of not eating meat on Fridays in Lent. But Aquinas believes that the word "abstinence" remains appropriate for this virtue because it represents the ability to abstain from excessive, inappropriate, or unhealthy eating. What the term probably doesn't capture for us today is the virtue's positive direction to prudent eating and to the real enjoyment of a good meal.

It is in this context that Aquinas speaks of the religious practice of fasting as an expression of the virtue of abstinence. Someone who is not more generally abstinent will find it difficult to fast. At the same time, the effort to fast (during Lent, for example) can help to build up the virtue of abstinence. Of course, even the praiseworthy spiritual practice of fasting must be guided by prudence.

The vice of gluttony is the acquired tendency to eat to excess, to eat unhealthy things, or to eat at inappropriate times and places. It also includes excessive pleasure in eating, or at least a disposition to choose foods solely for the pleasures they give without consideration of their healthiness. In our day, we know that there are many complex reasons that people might overeat—many of them not properly moral. Our culture gives us powerful but essentially mixed messages. On the one hand, there is a cult of physical fitness, beauty, and youth—and thus the constant marketing of foods, supplements, programs, devices, and the like, which purport to promote these benefits. On the other hand, there is the constant bombardment of advertising for fast food and other unhealthy choices, as well as "super-sized" meals. While today we should acknowledge the multilayered factors that impact our food choices, there remains for most of us the element of choice. One choice to eat poorly, one time after another, leads to the virtual inability to choose rightly, even when our health is at stake. In a similar way, we must not "shame" others or ourselves about our bodies or our eating;

but at the same time, we must take responsibility for the choices we can and do make.

Aquinas reminds his readers that gluttony is traditionally considered a "capital" sin—that is, other sins flow from it. It weakens us in our ability to act properly and moderately in respect to our desires more generally. It is no coincidence that an ancient remedy for unchastity is fasting. When one desire is out of control, others are easily impacted. On the other hand, to be able to moderate our desires in one area (eating) can help us to order our desires in another (sex). At the same time, as we all know from the "overstuffed" feeling that can follow a huge holiday meal, Aquinas says that gluttony dulls our minds. Focusing our attention inordinately to food and its pleasures, gluttony also can easily dull our desire for God and for the practice of prayer. Who wants to pray when they are stuffed? And who can pray when their desires are actively pulling them in other directions?

Temperance in Drinking

Following the words of the Book of Sirach, Aquinas believes that moderate consumption of alcohol is a good thing: "Wine is very life to human beings if taken in moderation. What is life to one who is without wine? It has been created to make people happy. Wine drunk at the proper time and in moderation is rejoicing of heart and gladness of soul" (Sir 31:27–28). Alcoholic beverages, in proper measure, can bring relaxation to individuals and enhance friendly social interaction. The First Letter to Timothy advocates a little wine as good for the stomach and other ailments (1 Tim 5:23). Aquinas calls the acquired tendency to moderation in drinking "sobriety," telling us that the word comes from a root that means "measure." It involves the ability to drink in moderation in the right circumstances and to refrain when appropriate.

The opposite of moderation in drinking is the vice of drunkenness. Again, just as Aquinas would have been unaware of the reality of eating disorders, so too he would not have been aware of the disease of alcoholism. He is addressing, rather, the moral reality of people who can but do not moderate their drinking. There are people who are not alcoholics but who regularly drink to excess, despite the inappropriate results. We see this sad reality, for example, in binge drinking on college campuses by young people who are not addicted to alcohol but intemperate in its use. Such intemperance is also a form of imprudence, as the sad and sometimes tragic consequences of drinking beyond one's capacity makes clear.

Temperance in Sex

The virtue of chastity is the habitual disposition to act moderately and appropriately in the use of our sexuality. The term, Aquinas notes, is related to the word "chastening" in the sense of rebuking our sinful tendencies, and indeed we can often experience the effort to grow in chastity in exactly that way. But Aquinas is not suggesting that chastity is essentially a negative or restraining virtue. Sexual desire in itself is good and natural; sexual activity in marriage is good; and the pleasure enjoyed during such sex is also good. Like all of the forms of temperance, it is a matter of moderation and balance—and ultimately what is truly good for the person and for other persons who are involved. Without the internal order and tranquility that chastity brings, we cannot truly recognize and value the true beauty of our own sexuality and the physical beauty of others. Without chastity, what is truly beautiful in itself is reduced by us in thought and action into a mere instrumental good for ourselves.

Aquinas makes a distinction between chastity and purity. Strictly speaking, chastity concerns good order in actual sex. Purity, on the other hand, concerns the thoughts and fantasies, conversations, and actions that lead up to and surround sexual union. But they are not separate virtues. Chastity is the virtue, and purity is its support or extension. While ultimately Aquinas himself does not really pursue the distinction, it does remind us of the broader range of chastity in its building up and manifestation.

Chastity, like all of the virtues, brings ease, smoothness, and promptitude in doing the good. The truly chaste person does not have to struggle to resist temptation and to do good. The ability to overcome temptation by strong effort is what Aquinas calls *continence*. It is a kind of imperfect or intermediate virtue at best, because it allows one to resist temptation, but without the tranquility and promptness of a true virtue. Continence can also be spoken of in regard to temperance in eating and drinking, as well as other virtues related to temperance, but perhaps its meaning is most obvious in regard to sex. Its opposite is incontinence. (In our contemporary usage, "incontinence" is more likely to refer to the inability to control one's bladder or bowels. In any case, the broad meaning is the same: the ability—or lack of it—to keep some desire or perceived need under control, perhaps at the cost of some effort.)

The opposite of chastity is the vice of lust. The unchaste person is habitually unable to resist their sexual desires, and thus acts in unhealthy or inappropriate ways with their sexuality in thought, word, or action. Aquinas notes that, like gluttony, lust is a capital sin in that it can impact us more broadly. The inability to properly direct and order any of our desires toward authentic goods and actions can easily promote imbalance in other areas as well.

Like all virtues, chastity must be guided by prudence. In different ages and cultures, what might constitute unchaste thoughts or even actions can be judged differently in specific situations. Today we see human sexuality in a more positive light and have greater understanding of its psychological and relational depth. Thus, the shape of what is thought to constitute chastity might develop, but it is nonetheless abundantly clear that it remains a virtue that is essential to the authentically human life well-lived in relation with others. Aquinas believed, as the Catholic tradition continues to hold, that there are expressions of our sexuality that truly serve our humanity and our relationships with others—and others that do not. This runs contrary to the widespread sense in our contemporary culture that sex means whatever a person or persons want it to mean. This is not the place for a full treatment of the virtue of chastity for today. It can only be noted that the real meaning of chastity can only be rightly understood in the context of an authentic sense of what human sexuality is.

Other Moderating Virtues

In addition to abstinence, sobriety, and chastity, which are forms of temperance in relation to different realms of desire, Aquinas identifies other related virtues that also moderate our desires and our external behavior.

Mildness and Clemency in the Face of Anger

For Aquinas, anger is a natural human passion. It can be good or bad. In fact, there are situations of evil or injustice in which anger is the appropriate reaction. It then serves as the power behind the courage which moves and directs us to overcome difficulties to restore justice or accomplish some difficult good. It can actually be wrong not to become angry in some circumstances. But, of course, it must be moderated. It must be a temperate anger, suited and proportioned to the evil and the circumstances and in the measure and type of response. As the psalmist says: "When you are disturbed [angry], do not sin" (Ps 4:5).

The principal problem, as we know from our experience, is inordinate anger that is out of balance, disproportionate, or misdirected. It often moves us to some form of revenge. As a vice, anger is not just a matter of an occasional outburst of anger, but rather a habit of responding to situations with an anger that is out of proportion to the perceived evil or injustice. Aquinas notes that anger sometimes takes the form of a tendency to erupt with anger, but it can also take the form of bitterness or sullenness in which one nurses one's anger. Or it can take the form of a general attitude of resentment or bad-temperedness.

Anger is traditionally considered a capital sin—that is, it is the headwaters of a river of other evil. It can lead, as Aquinas notes, to quarreling or physical altercations, hateful speech to or about others, or other acts of vengeance. But such anger is no less the source of suffering for the one who holds on to anger. The habit of harboring anger is usually more harmful to ourselves than the objects of our anger.

Aquinas uses the term "mildness" or "meekness" to describe the acquired tendency to moderate our anger. In our day, both terms seem to have more of connotation of being timid or submissive, and this is certainly not what Aquinas had in mind. Perhaps we might call the virtue "even-temperedness." The even-tempered person is not unable or unwilling to get angry, but rather is not controlled by inordinate anger.

Clemency, Aquinas says, is the moderation of anger when seeking retribution and in punishing. Someone who has been treated unjustly has a right to restitution or recompense, and the unjust person has a duty to give it. But the restitution or recompense expected must not be out of proportion to the wrong committed. When it is a matter of punishing, clemency is not necessarily the refusal to punish appropriately, but it is the acquired disposition to act without allowing anger to lead to excess. Parents and judges, for example, must have the virtue of clemency so that justice can be restored without excess. The opposite of clemency is cruelty, which leads one to inflict excessive or injurious punishment. And beyond the pale of cruelty is brutality, or savagery, which is indifferent to innocence or guilt, and is willing to inflict harm indiscriminately. We can think of modern-day terrorists in this context.

Modesty

For Aquinas, modesty is a broad-ranging virtue that regulates other human desires, less urgent or less immediately physical than our desires for food, drink, and sex. In some of its forms, it moderates our internal attitudes, and in others our external behaviors. In its different species or contexts, it brings proper order to our desire and striving to excel, our desire to gain knowledge, our desire for play and diversion, and our desire for maintaining a good appearance. Thus, for Aquinas, modesty includes what we might think of today as prudence in the manner of dress, but its range is considerably more extensive.

Humility

At first glance, it might seem odd to consider humility as a form of modesty in its relation to temperance. Rather, it might seem more aptly related to the virtue of justice, giving to people (including ourselves) what is duly owed. In that light, the attempt to appear better than we are or to receive more praise than we are due would be a kind of injustice, a failure in truth-telling about ourselves. But Aquinas sees humility as a form of modesty, in that it is the virtue that regulates our desire to attain, achieve, and excel. There is nothing inherently wrong with such desires, but they must be regulated in relation to reality—to the truth of our capacities and what we have truly attained (or could reasonably hope to accomplish).

Saint Teresa of Avila spoke of humility as "walking in truth"—living in the truth of who we are. This is very much in keeping with Saint Thomas's thought here. As human beings, we have a natural desire to achieve—each of us according to our gifts and opportunities. But that desire must be regulated by the constant recognition that every personal gift is really a gift of God. It must be moderated too by an honest appraisal of our real capacities, even as we might appropriately strive to push our limits. Our actual attainments and our ongoing desire to achieve must not lead us to overrate those prior achievements or lead others to do so. In our common way of saying things, we might say of a great athlete, artist, or scholar that she shows a great deal of humility or modesty in regard to what she has accomplished, not merely as an external pose, but as an abiding attitude with its accompanying comportment.

Pride is the vice that is opposed to humility. It is our desire to achieve being out of touch with reality and the truth of who and what we are. Pride is the disposition to think of ourselves as more than we are, to overestimate and overly esteem our capacities and accomplishments. It inclines us to think that we possess gifts that we do not have—or that we do not possess to the degree that we would like to think. It disposes us to think of ourselves as better than others, and sometimes to appear to others as better than we are or better than others (though Aquinas refers more specifically to the desire to appear more accomplished than we are as "vainglory"). With the eyes of faith, it is the tendency to be blind to the divine role in the gifts we have and our ability to develop them. Pride thereby leads to the illusion that we can be autonomous of or self-sufficient without God. It is in this context that Aquinas speaks of the pride and the sin of Adam and Eve.

In considering the virtue of fortitude, we saw that magnanimity is a virtue that "thinks big" about what can be accomplished and that acknowledges our real capacities to attain great things. As we saw, it is related to courage, in that the ability to aspire to great things in keeping with one's abilities enables one to overcome obstacles to the attainment of great things. It is magnanimity's ability to think big that empowers a magnanimous person to accomplish great and worthy ends. At the same time, it is precisely in magnanimity's realistic acknowledgement of our actual capacities that allows it to coexist with the virtue of humility. Authentic humility is not opposed to magnanimity; but, with its eye on the truth of one's capacities, it prevents magnanimity from becoming pride or vainglory. It is not authentically humble to underestimate one's gifts any more than it is to overestimate them.

Studiousness and Idle Curiosity

The desire to seek knowledge is an important human trait. Without it, human beings could not have advanced as a species. Discoveries in science, medicine, and technology are rooted in the basic human desire to know. We naturally want to know about ourselves, about the world around us, what makes things work, and how to make things better.

Studiousness (*studiositas*) is the virtue that moderates our desire to know. It is virtuous to have a developed desire to seek knowledge that is good and true and that can benefit the self and others. As the English term suggests, it is not the mere acknowledgement that we must sometimes seek some immediate knowledge to solve a particular problem or do well on an exam. A studious person is disposed to seek out knowledge, not only for its immediate and practical value, but also for higher values to the self and others. At the same time, the virtue moderates such desire, since it is not always good and appropriate to seek knowledge. There are other, sometimes more important and urgent, goods to be sought.

Curiosity, in our contemporary way of speaking, can be a positive value—an important aspect of the desire to know. Aquinas speaks, however, of the vice that he calls *curiositas*. We might call it "idle" or "excessive" curiosity. We know that people can be excessively curious, interested in knowing things that are really none of their business and not their right to know. Some people are nosy—always interested in the business of others. Aquinas notes that people can have the bad tendency to seek a type of knowledge that it is bad in itself, for the purpose of seeking bad ends, or that is simply useless. We can seek knowledge that is not our business for the sake of passing on gossip, making ourselves feel superior to those about whom we have gained some knowledge, or simply to store it away for some future purpose. This is not a matter of legitimate personal interests and hobbies, but of the desire for knowledge that is excessive, bad, wasteful, or selfish. It can be the sign of a restless and unsettled mind and spirit.

Perhaps one of the contemporary forms of *curiositas* is found in the endless ability that we now have to waste time in gaining useless knowledge. Some people are addicted to the news and endless, repetitive commentaries by "talking heads" on CNN, FOX, or MSNBC. Others can idle away hours watching the Weather Channel to gain knowledge of storms and weather conditions that will not impact them, and about which they cannot do anything. It is easy enough to be caught up in one Google search after another or in the continuous move from one "interesting" web link to another. (Young people today speak of FOMO—fear of missing out.) With the sheer quantity of information now available to us through the Internet, we need the virtue of *studiositas* more than ever to moderate our desire to know and channel it in important and useful directions, in keeping with other legitimate demands on our time and attention.

Proper Order in Personal Comportment

For Aquinas, modesty is a virtue in itself that moderates our external behaviors and appearance, conforming them to what is appropriate and fitting to ourselves and our current circumstances. Modest behavior is prudent behavior. To some degree, it is about good manners and an easy sociability. As we saw in speaking of virtues related to justice, there are virtues that are focused on a life in community which is more convivial and thus more human. An external modesty in behavior is, of course, grounded in the proper order of our interior desires. It is the virtue of modesty that directs the inner movements that manifest themselves in action.

Our external behaviors have direct impact on others; and so, modesty—as the virtue that moderates our behaviors—is related to friendliness or affability, which are in turn related to justice. In this regard, the modest person is disposed to act in a way that is appropriate and, where possible, pleasing to others. Obviously, this is not a way that we would speak about modesty today. But Aquinas is telling us that we need a virtue that will guide and order our social interactions, not only in matters that concern justice itself, but that insure that our conversation, our comportment, and our manner of relating are fitting. Perhaps this point becomes clearer when we think of people who don't seem to pick up on social cues, who are boorish, who don't have a good sense of what is appropriate to say or do in different situations when relating with different people.

Modesty is a virtue that moderates our external behavior, but it also directs the person to an accurate consistency or authenticity between our outward actions and words and the truth of our inner attitudes. Our actions and behaviors must not only be appropriate but authentic. It is not virtuous to know how to charm people by deceiving them or merely appearing as one thinks they want. It is immodest, in that sense, to make a pretense of feelings or attitudes that one does not in fact experience. In this regard, modesty is related to truthfulness and opposed to dissimulation.

Good Balance in Play and Diversion

The human body, Aquinas prudently observes, needs adequate rest. In the same way, the human soul needs rest, and this takes the form of play or other forms of diversion and fun. Saint Thomas is no dour ascetic or overly cerebral academic. Relaxation and play are good. Seeking out some healthy fun and diversion is good for the person and for his or her social relations. Of course, the virtue disposes the person to moderation: not too little play, not too much nor the wrong kind.

Perhaps it is clearer in our age that someone can lack virtue in this area by being disposed to too little play. Some people are workaholics, driven beyond real necessity to earn, accomplish, and do. But play is part of a fully human life and part of healthy relationships and families. It is a vice not to find balance where it can be found. A life without appropriate play easily becomes mirthless and bland. Such a life would lack, as Aquinas reminds us, what Aristotle called *eutrapelia*, the virtue of wittiness or cheerfulness. In fact, Saint Thomas points to lack of mirth as a vice that hinders the joy of others and makes one's presence burdensome to them rather than enjoyable.

Probably more obvious is the possibility of too much play or the wrong kind of diversion. Good play cannot be injurious to others, immoral or indecent in itself. We ought not to engage in good diversions if we give them more time than is appropriate to our lives and other responsibilities. There is nothing inherently wrong in playing video games (at least if they aren't too violent or indecent), watching TV or YouTube videos, or surfing the Internet. But it is a matter of time and energy devoted to such pastimes in relationship to our life circumstances and the proper demands of our important relationships. Moreover, Aquinas cautions that the good of humor and jesting among friends can be marred by failing to take into proper account the feelings of the people involved and the circumstances. This is another way of saying, again, that healthy play must be guided by prudence and by justice in relation to others.

Modesty in Dress

When we think of modesty in dress, we probably immediately think of the need to dress in a manner that is not too revealing, overtly sexual, or directed to incite lust in others. And Saint Thomas does include this sense of the word in speaking of the virtue of modesty. But the need to moderate our external appearance—and the inner desires that direct our choices— is much broader. Appropriate dress must also not be extravagant, merely showy, or designed to promote vanity. On the other hand, the virtue of modesty in dress demands that our attire not be slovenly or dirty. The point here is not merely about fashion or fussiness in dress but rather an external demeanor that reflects a balanced and mature person who is able to intuit what is appropriate to different contexts. Aquinas is explicitly aware that questions of dress vary according to circumstances and customs. His concern is our ability to exercise prudent good order in our external as well as our internal lives.

Conclusion

In our day, the word "temperance" can conjure up images of puritanical people seeking to ban drinking or people who are prudish, straight-laced, or scrupulous. The idea of "mastering" or even "controlling" desire can seem, to contemporary sensibilities, necessarily suspicious of desire or pleasure. Temperance might seem to suggest repression. But, as we have seen in these pages, Saint Thomas Aquinas holds no such view of the virtue of temperance nor, by extension, of desire and pleasure. Desires are part of being human. They direct us to things that are good for us, and the pleasure in attaining such goods is also good.

Desire is part of being human, but it is not the whole picture. We also have our intellect's ability to see what is truly good for self and others, not merely pleasurable for me, here and now. And we have the ability of the will to decide rightly how we will act on what we desire and what we perceive to be the true good in any particular situation. But also part of every human life is the reality of sin. "Disordered concupiscence" is a result of original sin that involves an inherent tendency within us to disordered desire. It is not yet sin, but a tendency to it. Our own history of personal sin—our history of disordered choices and our actual vices—can then pull us further in directions that will not serve out authentic development and living. Social sin, as it has become embedded in the world around us, provides a constant temptation to choices that are neither appropriate nor ultimately healthy for ourselves and those around us.

The virtue of temperance, for Aquinas, directs us to the proper coming together of desiring, the use of our intellect, and right choosing. Fundamentally, it moves us to a proper balancing within ourselves so that we can be and function as human persons ought, precisely and distinctively as our authentically-lived human nature directs. Temperance orders us from within so that we can act rightly outside ourselves. It is the habitual tendency to seek the balance and inner tranquility which is central to living consistently in a manner truly worthy of the human person.

6

The Christian Life of Virtue

EXAMINING THE CARDINAL AND related virtues in the thought of Saint Thomas Aquinas, we have been considering those dispositions and attitudes that make us better human beings and that allow us to live a life that is more truly worthy of the human person. We are better people because we are prudent, just, courageous, and temperate. The choices and actions that flow from these dispositions are good—good for those impacted by our actions and good for ourselves as their agents. And, when individuals grow in these virtues and act in good ways, they contribute to relationships and communities that are also more authentically human and worthy of human beings. And such communities, in turn, contribute to the formation of men and women of sturdy virtue.

Aquinas's teaching on these natural, moral virtues offers us important lessons for our life in the contemporary world. Today, many in our society no longer believe that we can speak of moral rules or principles that apply to all people in at least virtually all circumstances. The idea that there is a "natural law"—the foundation of traditional Catholic moral teaching—is suspect to a significant number of people, including those who self-identify as Catholic. At one time, we could speak of a shared "Judeo-Christian" heritage that included some shared sense of morality and of prohibited actions. Without such a basic moral sensibility, we must still find common moral ground in order to live together in society. In the context of our world today, the ability to appeal to a shared sense of the moral dispositions that should mark a good human life and a good human community would be no small accomplishment. In the end, we still might not reach the same conclusions about specific moral actions, but we would be a lot closer to some level of moral consensus in society. The teaching of Aquinas on virtue has a great deal to recommend it to us as human persons and as a society.

But this is not to say that he would have been content to leave it at that. For Aquinas, the virtues as good dispositions are very much tied to an objective moral order in which some things are right or wrong, regardless of an individual's sincere belief about them. But more to our purposes in this book, for Saint Thomas, the natural moral virtues on their own can lead only to a kind of provisional, imperfect human excellence. His was a profoundly theological view of human life in general and of the moral life in particular. With the vision of Christian faith, Saint Thomas believed that, created in the image of God and made for divine union, we cannot reach our fullest development as humans except in relationship with God. The life truly worthy of the human person is life directed to and lived in divine communion. The apex of human community is sharing together in the life of the Persons of the Trinity.

For the Christian, the natural moral virtues—as essential as they are—do not tell the whole story. We also need virtues given to us by God, which do not eliminate our human virtues but allow them to attain their fullest form as directed to our union with God. For the Christian, the cardinal and related virtues do not have an existence within us independent of our relationship with the divine. Although the focus of this book has been the cardinal virtues, we cannot conclude our reflection without looking at where Saint Thomas himself actually begins: with the ultimate fulfillment of the human person in God and the virtues which are "infused"—poured into us—by God so that we can reach that lofty goal.

Ultimate Human Fulfillment and Happiness

For Aquinas, all human life and every human person has a goal. We are all inherently directed to our own authentic and ultimate fulfillment as human persons. Whether we are conscious of it or not, all of us are seeking our own fulfillment in every choice we make. We can call this fulfillment by the name "happiness," but our truest life goal as human persons is not happiness in a superficial or incomplete way. Human life is aimed at that ultimate happiness which will be found only when we are most truly who and what we were meant to be as human persons. The natural human virtues that we have been discussing lead us, as we have seen, to a kind of human excellence, a fulfillment of what it means to be truly human in this world. But such excellence and this-worldly fulfillment as persons necessarily remains imperfect because our ultimate completion lies beyond anything that we can accomplish on our own in this life.

Following the creation story in Genesis (1:26–27), Aquinas (and the Catholic tradition with him) believed that the human person is created in the image of God. We are made in the divine image, and we are made for union with God. Therefore, we can only become who and what we were meant to be—most authentically human—when we are one with God. To be human is to have an infinite capacity for union with God—a destiny and a potential so lofty that it surpasses our unaided ability to realize. The reality of sin has further obstructed any possible realization of this goal by our own effort. But that which should be impossible for us is now made possible by the incarnation and saving death and resurrection of Christ. The power of sin is destroyed, and our humanity is renewed and elevated. And now, the church and its teaching, our sharing in its sacramental life, and prayer and other spiritual practices in the life of the Christian community are all aids in attaining our fulfillment: life together in and with God.

We, of course, have our own role to play, transformed through baptism and aided by God's gracious presence. And the virtues are a central element in our part in the attainment of our ultimate fulfillment. The virtues, as we have seen, guide and form our natural capacities (which Aquinas identifies as our intellect, will, and sense appetites) so that we can arrive at a true, if incomplete, human excellence. The natural virtues are precisely the habitual dispositions, developed over time by our choices (always aided by grace), that enable us (together, teaches Aquinas, with law and grace) to perform good actions and to avoid evil. Fundamentally transformed by our baptism into Christ, our natural virtues do not lose their importance, nor are they left behind. Rather, these natural virtues are taken up into the completion of our life journey in God, which can only be accomplished by the further work of grace and the divine gift of the theological and other infused virtues. Our natural virtues—and our graced effort to develop them—become part of God's greater work in fulfilling our true destiny as human persons created in the divine image.

Theological Virtues

We are not capable of good action apart from the grace of God. Even growth in the natural moral virtues requires the divine help. But the infused virtues come to us directly from God as a gift. These dispositions are "poured into us" (infused) by God, and they can also be called supernatural virtues as distinct from the natural virtues that we have been examining in previous chapters. We must claim them, embrace them, and nurture their growth within us; but we cannot produce them in ourselves. First and foremost among these God-given virtues are the theological virtues of faith, hope, and charity.

We are accustomed to being assured of the closeness of God, of God's love for us, and of the divine presence in the Spirit. God holds us in existence at every moment and, in this sense, is present to us at the most fundamental level of our being. We know that God calls us into relationship and invites us to share in eternal life (all of which is, of course, profoundly true). But perhaps we don't often think about the fact that all of this is only possible because of God's constant and renewed initiative and gift. Although God has created us and loves us with an immense love, there remains an infinite distance between God and us at a fundamental level. We are not capable, on our part alone, of entering into divine relationship, much less entering into union with God. This possibility comes to us through the wonder of the incarnation and the death and resurrection of Christ, by which the Son of God took on our humanity, bridged the infinite gap between us and God, and destroyed the alienating power of sin. Claiming and living this miraculous possibility is the wonder of the theological virtues given to us by God in Christ through the working of the Spirit.

On our own, we are not capable of coming to know God and truths about God. God must give us the gift of the theological virtue of faith for such knowledge. We would have no reason to expect to attain union with God, except that God gives us the hope that it is within our grasp, and that the divine help will not fail us along the way. We are not capable of embracing the divine self-giving love, nor of returning a true self-gift to God—the virtue of charity—unless it comes first as a divine gift.

The theological virtues relate us directly to God, and so they lead us to our true fulfillment in divine communion. Faith, hope, and charity don't eliminate the cardinal and related virtues. Rather, they give them their full meaning and scope; the acquired virtues are "taken up" by the theological virtues. Now, it must be said that, in actual living, it is not as if we grow in the cardinal virtues and then are ready to "graduate" to theological virtues. We don't develop the virtues of prudence, justice, courage, and temperance and then move on to faith, hope, and love. In traditional terms, the theological virtues come with grace—with being in a "state of grace"—and therefore in the actual unfolding of the Christian life in a person baptized as an infant, they are prior to, empowering of, and formative for the growth of the moral virtues. In fact, in actual living, we are constantly striving to embrace and nurture the theological virtues, even as we endeavor to grow in their natural, acquired counterparts.

Although the theological virtues come as a divine gift, Aquinas teaches that they are truly virtues in that they are abiding habits that direct our actions. It is true that we cannot acquire them on our own; but, at the same time, we must embrace the divine gift and nurture these virtues within ourselves in our choices and actions. We can look, for example, at a person who is able to remain positive and strong in their faith through great hardship and think: "Wow, she has a lot of faith. I wish that I had faith like that." But it's not that God generally hands out greater faith to one than another. It's just that some people embrace and nurture their faith from day to day in the decisions that they make. When they need that faith, in the sense of maintaining it and growing in it through tough times, it is available to them. On the other hand, if we have not nurtured our faith by such things as prayer, sacraments, and spiritual reading, we ought not to be surprised if, in the face of great hardship, we seem to lack faith or feel in danger of losing it.

The Virtue of Faith

Christian faith is the virtue by which we come to know God and truths about God, especially as these are revealed to us in the Word of God, and specifically in Jesus Christ. It is an abiding acceptance by our minds of a type of knowing that is not the result of our simple observations or reasoning. Such knowledge is not contrary to what we can know by our natural thinking, but it concerns things that are beyond our intellect's grasp. In faith, we believe that there is a God; we believe that God, especially in Jesus, is the fundamental truth of reality and of our human existence; and we believe that, again especially in Jesus, God reveals to us the way to live and to attain our eternal salvation. Because of what we know in faith, we come to trust, surrender, and seek an ever-deepening relationship with God in this life and in the next. More broadly, therefore, faith is a way of knowing, it is believing and belief, and it is trust and relationship with God. We see more clearly that mature Christian faith is intimately linked with the relationship of friendship with God which Aquinas believes is the central meaning of charity.

It is the light of faith, shining on the life and teaching of Jesus, that reveals the true contours of authentic human living, and thus the authentic shape of all of the virtues. The virtue of faith is, then, an abiding way of knowing and a sustained way of seeing God, self, other people, relationships, the created order, what constitutes authentic value, and what counts as worthy priorities. In faith, we see differently which goals are worthy of our pursuit and more urgent in attaining. In light of the life and teaching of Jesus, as it is passed on in the church, we consider in new ways which possible means of attaining our goals are truly appropriate and worthy. In every situation, we are enlightened to see other persons as brothers and sisters to us and equally worthy of our consideration and concern. We have a wider picture of what constitutes essential sources of counsel and guidance for our decision-making. In short, embracing and deepening the virtue of faith must necessarily shape the virtue of prudence.

We can see that the same is true for the impact of faith on justice, fortitude, temperance and their related virtues. The abiding knowledge and vision of faith changes our view of the nature, depth, and breadth of our responsibilities to and for other human beings. It widens our sense of the goals that are worthy of our pursuit even in the face of great difficulty and gives us new motivation and power to pursue them. It gives us a more magnanimous soul, yet bigger dreams and nobler goals, and a far greater reason for confidence in what can and should be accomplished. Because faith directs us toward a more transcendent goal for our lives—even as it leaves us firmly planted in this life as we find it—it redirects our desiring and understands differently what constitutes good measure and balance in our lives.

The Virtue of Hope

The theological virtue of hope is the abiding expectation that we can attain union with God and that God will give us the means and the help to do so. It is in the coming of Jesus, in his teachings and promises, and especially in his saving death and resurrection that we come to the surest hope. To know in faith who God is and to expect in hope to be with God awakens a deeper aspiration and resolve to set out, remain firm, and reach out for the divine assistance along the path. Hope doesn't eliminate the recognition that our goal can be difficult to attain, and it certainly doesn't mean that we won't have our struggles along the way. But hope is what sees us through, opens us to God's promised help, and keeps us faithfully on course, whatever may come.

Hope, born of faith and its distinctive vision, empowers us to see the present with an eye to the future. Hope in what God has promised and in the divine reign to come in its fullness unsettles our easy satisfaction in what we have and presently are, challenges us to see beyond the difficulties of the present, and empowers us to be agents of change in the world around us and in our lives and hearts. Again, the cardinal and their related virtues are further enlivened and shaped by hope. What is to be prudently pursued looks different in light of hope's vision of the world to come and with expectation of what God can accomplish in and through us. Hope in God does not, by any means, eliminate the need for prudence; but the hope-filled form of the virtue is a prudence that sees worthier goals and new channels of (divine) assistance in their attainment. Hope unsettles our sense of contentment in the status quo of the world around us and sees new possibilities that justice alone cannot see. Hope gives new power to courage and worthier goals to pursue, even as it brings renewed and integrating desire for what God has promised and what God can do.

The Virtue of Charity

Saint Thomas tells us that the theological virtue of charity is friendship with God. The Scriptures make clear that, from the very beginning, God has invited men and women into intimate relationship. But there always remained the distance between the infinite God and the finite creature, as well as the obstacle of sin and its consequences. It is God who had to bridge the gap in order to make true friendship possible between divine and human. And so, in the incarnation by which God became human and through the reconciling action of Jesus in the cross and resurrection, friendship with God is made possible. God "comes down," as it were; and, through baptism and the life of grace, we are raised up into friendship with God. Charity is the virtue by which we are able to receive God's self-giving love and return that love in our own self-giving response.

In charity, we love God, and we love those God has created who bear the divine image and who are loved by God. For Aquinas, love of God and neighbor—as well as an authentic love for self—are fundamentally one love. They are inseparable. The Gospel and Letters of John make this abundantly clear: "Those who say, 'I love God,' and hate their brothers or sisters, are liars; for those who do not love a brother or sister whom they have seen, cannot love God whom they have not seen. The commandment we have from him is this: those who love God must love their brothers and sisters also" (1 John 4:20–21).

Charity is most clearly related to the virtue of justice. The virtue of justice moves us habitually to give to others what is owed to them. Charity moves us to give yet more than what is demanded in justice, because we come to realize a deeper and more profound bond with other persons as our brothers and sisters and as the beloved of God, created in the divine image. Charity is that friendship with God that reaches out in pursuit of friendship—the reciprocity of love—with other persons. Therefore, it necessarily transforms justice's more narrow and restricted sense of relationship and mutual responsibilities. Justice, on its own, looks to give worldly, natural goods to others. Charity looks beyond to what God wants for all of us: our truest fulfillment together in union with the Trinity. Charity, then, "takes up" justice and moves us beyond "mere" justice; but charity does not thereby eliminate the virtue of justice, nor the need to pursue justice. Charity requires at least justice, and is not exhausted by it. But without justice, there can be no real charity.

Charity, teaches Saint Thomas, can increase in this life, not by adding "more," but by becoming more intense. We can grow in our friendship with God, in our openness to receive and to give to God and to our sisters and brothers. This intensifying charity becomes, as Aquinas says it, the "form of the virtues." By this, he means that when we have received the gift of the theological virtue of charity, it comes to fill, empower, shape, and direct all of our virtues to God. When we have charity, we live our life directed toward God, our ultimate end, and true fulfillment. And in this fundamental life direction and relationship, all of our other attitudes and dispositions come to be integrated and empowered. The natural, moral virtues attain their truest shape and completion.

Infused Moral Virtues

Saint Thomas teaches that, in addition to the theological virtues, God infuses moral virtues, which are parallel to our natural, acquired virtues, and so there are both natural and infused forms of each of the cardinal virtues. Fundamentally, this teaching is grounded in Aquinas's thoroughly theological vision of the moral life, and more specifically in his view of the Christian life as a life lived in and empowered by grace. Through incorporation into Christ through baptism, thus filled with the divine presence in grace, we are truly transformed. In this sense, the infused moral virtues aren't "add-ons" or supplements to a separate "natural" moral life. Rather, they are the divine gifts by which God enables the full unfolding of our humanity, including through our acquired moral virtues. The infused moral virtues, then, are not some parallel reality superimposed over our own moral dispositions. They are what animate, shape, and strengthen our dispositions and actions through our natural powers of intellect and will so that we can act in accord with the divine will for ourselves and for the world—which is to say, for our true good and for the good of those around us.

Ideally, our acquired and infused moral virtues work together. But this is not necessarily so; and examining this possibility can help us to understand the difference between them. Let's say that I have developed the vice of back-biting (contrary to the virtue of justice)—that is, I have the nasty habit of gossiping about others behind their backs. I sincerely repent, confess my sin, and receive sacramental absolution. I leave the sacrament washed clean and renewed. With the new outpouring of grace, I receive the infused moral virtue of justice in speech about others. But, at a natural level, I still have the acquired vice of back-biting—the habitual disposition to speak ill of others behind their backs. I must work to overcome this vice. The infused moral virtue, as the abiding fruit of grace at work in my will, will help. Further, with the expansive vision of faith, infused justice in speech will offer me an expanded vision of the people about whom I might be tempted to speak—seeing them as truly brothers and sisters to me. It will give me a deeper love of truth as a reflection of God who is truth, and it will have a deeper appreciation of the relationship of my actions with my hope of union with God.

The infused moral virtues work in our natural faculties, as do the acquired virtues; but in their supernatural form, they may alter the operation of their acquired counterparts. Natural prudence and justice, for example, move us to act with a healthy concern for ourselves and others in the realm of normal human living. But infused prudence moves us to see our decisions in a larger perspective—with the eyes of faith—taking into account supernatural ends. With infused prudence, a young man or woman might rightly consider leaving a high-paying job and the promise of financial success to pursue a life of ministry. From a merely human prudence, the same decision might seem very imprudent indeed. Of course, infused prudence is still prudence. It must take into account many factors and possible consequences for multiple people. Infused prudence in this example does not replace or nullify acquired prudence. It takes it up and includes it, but places its considerations into a bigger or deeper perspective.

In the same way, while natural justice aims to give to others what is due to them, the infused virtue of justice sees a bigger picture of what we owe to others, including those things that would serve their spiritual welfare (and especially regarding those near and dear to us). Infused courage sees the goals that are worthy of sacrifice differently. And so we have not only the courage of soldiers who are willing to face death in order to protect their nation and its citizens, but we also have the courage of martyrs who face death for something intangible and transcendent, yet profoundly real and infinitely precious—eternal life. While acquired temperance moves us to healthy eating and proper sleep, infused temperance sees the value of occasional fasting and vigils. In short, the infused virtues are based on a faith vision that sees the human good more completely and so directs us to our true fulfillment as persons.

Gifts of the Holy Spirit

In addition to the theological and infused moral virtues, Aquinas teaches that the gifts of the Holy Spirit make us more docile to the promptings of grace. The seven gifts are wisdom, understanding, counsel, fortitude, knowledge, piety, and fear of the Lord. The theological and other infused virtues are gifts from God but operate within our own graced capacities, but the gifts of the Holy Spirit make us immediately open to the movements of the Spirit. In this way, they complete and perfect the virtues under the divine inspiration of the Holy Spirit. In fact, in the course of his reflection on the virtues, Aquinas assigns a gift to each theological and cardinal virtue as its particular source of completion. Such is the comprehensive and systematizing mind of Saint Thomas.

Divine and Human, Personal and Communal

Saint Thomas's teaching on the infused and acquired virtues manifests the interconnection of divine action and human cooperation. God initiates, but we must respond. God offers; we must accept. At the same time, we must exert our own effort, but at the initiation and with the divine assistance. God loves and wills the ultimate happiness of all, but the divine love respects our freedom so that our response can truly be our own. In the divine plan, we need the gift of the theological and other infused virtues; and, at the same time, we need to exert our own effort in order to develop the acquired virtues, which will be taken up and perfected by the infused virtues. We must, with God's help and with our own graced effort, choose our own fulfillment in divine union.

Aquinas provides his lengthy and profound teaching on the virtues and the moral life more generally in the second part of his three-part *ST*. In the first part, he had discussed God, creation, the human, and the divine governance. In the third part, he moves on to discuss the saving work of Christ and the sacraments. (In fact, Saint Thomas died without having completed the *ST*, and some of his students prepared what is now called the Supplement, which concludes his teaching on specific sacraments and the life to come after death.) This arrangement is traditionally understood to reflect a vision of life as coming forth from God and our response (or return) to God through the moral life and the sacramental and spiritual life. The virtues, infused and acquired, fit into the divine plan by which we respond and return to God.

Since we depend so essentially on divine gift and aid, it becomes clear immediately why growth in virtue depends on prayer. The infused virtues come as gifts, an unfolding of God's own gracious presence. Our embrace of these gifts and the intensity of our acceptance of them depends on the openness to God that is the essence of prayer. At the same time, even the hard work of growing in the acquired virtues is dependent on the grace that empowers us and sustains us in the task. And so too, the acquired virtues are supported by prayer in their development, strengthening, and acting. It is in personal prayer and in communal prayer, especially in the sacramental life of the church, that we become more docile and receptive to the divine help and gift. As prayer (and thus, our relationship with God) deepens, our transformation in Christ becomes more profound and widens to new areas, with greater vigor and understanding. The more regular and profound our encounter and communion with God in Christ, the more we are able to embrace the infused virtues and to build our natural virtues.

But, at the same time, it must be said that the life of deep and sustained prayer can only grow in the soil prepared by the life of virtue. This is most evident in the case of the theological virtues, which are the divine gifts by which we are directed to God. Prayer, as we have seen, can be understood as an act of the natural virtue of religion; but the real depth of prayer depends on the relationship with God made possible and dynamic through grace and the theological virtues. The acquired virtues, for their part, order our desiring, our choices, our fundamental attitudes and dispositions, and so our relationships and way of being, so that we can find within ourselves the inner harmony and balance which deep prayer requires. We cannot truly encounter God and deepen our friendship with the divine when our actions, priorities, and attitudes run contrary to the divine will and being. But even more deeply, the virtues order our intellect and will, as well as our desiring as directed by them, and only in that way can we truly and deeply respond to God with the true depth of our freedom in our prayerful self-surrender to God, as well as in our choosing and acting.

Prayer and virtue must walk hand-in-hand. They depend on one another. They enrich one another. Each cannot truly exist without the other. Growing in virtues, acquired and infused, depends on the grace that becomes more effective through the receptivity of deepening prayer. Growth in prayer and in union with God depends on a life more and more conformed to God in our interior dispositions and in our external relationships and choices.

To acknowledge the necessity of communal, sacramental prayer, as well as personal prayer, reminds us that we are relational beings. The life of Christian faith is a communal reality. Our personal prayer in Christ always exists in the context of the praying church—the body of Christ, of which we are members. And so too, the life of virtues, infused and acquired, exists in the context of relationships and communities around us. Men and women, living the life of virtue, form human communities more worthy of human persons. Virtuous people make for communities of virtue, and communities of virtue form virtuous people. We are aided by the example of others, whether these are the living human beings we see around us, or the saints who have passed to the next life but who live with us still. As Christians, we see that growth in virtues, acquired and infused, requires our active participation in the life and prayer of the living Christian community, animated by the Spirit and centered in Christ.

The virtuous lives of Jesus, the Blessed Virgin, and the saints guide us and encourage us. The example and counsel of good people around us in the context of the community of faith fortify us, as we hope that our lives will do for them. Christian parents, grandparents, and other elders mentor us. The teachers in the church instruct us. The rich stories, powerful images, challenging parables, and wise teachings of the Scriptures form us. The liturgical and devotional life and prayer of the church nurture us. The sacraments sustain us. And, for our part, through our active participation in the life of the church, we contribute to the virtuous and prayerful lives of our sisters and brothers.

In the World in Which God Has Placed Us

The natural moral virtues which have been the principal focus of this book can be fully understood only in the larger picture of the Christian life. And yet they are a distinct element of the Christian and human life well-lived. Studying them separately, as Aquinas did and as we have done, gives us a clearer picture of the path to our fullest humanity. To say that there is a larger picture does not lessen the value of a more narrow examination of essential foundations of the moral life.

Christians today do not live in a Christian ghetto, cut off from the larger society which is no longer fundamentally Christian. Our world today is characterized by pluralism at virtually every level. We Christians live in the contemporary world as the leaven and witnesses of the reign of God, which God will finally and ultimately bring about. We must strive to be witnesses to the good news. The Catholic vision, as the Second Vatican Council made clear, is a life of active engagement in the world and participation in shared efforts to make the world more worthy of our humanity.

We must live in the world as it is and in dialogue with those around us in order to contribute to a shared life that is more authentically human. The fact that people are not Christian in no way denies that they can in fact live a more authentically human life than those who claim Christian faith. It is abundantly clear that people without Christian faith and with no religious faith at all can be women and men of profound natural virtue, solid good intention, and concrete action for the good of others. We Christians can often learn from them, even though we believe that the most authentic vision of what it means to be human and to serve the true good of other persons cannot be attained without faith.

Many older readers of this book (like its author) grew up in a society in which people believed that some actions are right or wrong regardless of anyone's opinion about them—actions like direct abortion and sex outside of marriage. In other words, we say that people used to believe in "objective truth" and "objective good." But the world has changed. Younger readers of this book have grown up in a world in which what is right depends on the views of the individual person performing any particular action. In view of a majority in our society, it is no longer possible to say that sex outside of marriage is simply wrong. Rather, it depends on how the two "consenting adults" view the meaning of their action. In other words, it is a world of "subjectivism" in which each subject largely determines what is right or wrong for him or herself.

While it is true that Aquinas's teaching on the virtues presupposes belief in an objective order and a larger vision of what leads us to authentic human fulfillment, his teaching on acquired virtues can be a bridge to moral consensus in our pluralistic society. In its foundation, his understanding of virtue is rooted in ancient Greek philosophy, which sought to promote a good human society comprised of people of virtue. Even if Christian faith suggests that the vision of pagan philosophers was necessarily incomplete, we cannot deny their fundamental human genius. Our goal may be the transformation of the world in and for Christ, but agreement on the dispositions that should mark good human persons and healthy human interactions would be no small human achievement in line with that more transcendent goal.

The effort to promote men and women of solid virtue, working for a society which is more worthy of human persons, is a profoundly Christian task. As we keep our eyes on the fullest picture of what our humanity means, we can also offer Saint Thomas Aquinas's Christian and human vision of the human life of virtue as an important contribution to the task. Our own efforts as women and men of virtue in our lives and in the little worlds in which we actually live is the proper task of the followers of Jesus, truly divine and extraordinarily human.

Bibliography

Aquinas, Thomas. *Summa Theologica*. Translated by the Fathers of the English Dominican Province. 3 vols. Westminster, MD: Christian Classics, 1981.

Cessario, Romanus. *The Moral Virtues and Theological Ethics*. Notre Dame: University of Notre Dame Press, 2009.

———. *The Virtues, or the Examined Life*. AMATECA Handbooks of Catholic Theology. New York: Continuum, 2002.

Donovan, Jean. *The Seven Virtues: An Introduction to Catholic Life*. New York: Crossroad, 2007.

Elders, Leo. J. *The Ethics of St. Thomas Aquinas: Happiness, Natural Law, and the Virtues*. New York: Peter Lang, 2005.

Finley, Mitch. *The Catholic Virtues: Seven Pillars of a Good Life*. Liguori, MO: Liguori, 1999.

Gratsch, Edward J. *Aquinas' Summa: An Introduction and Interpretation*. New York: Alba House, 1985.

Groeschel, Benedict. *The Virtue Driven Life*. Huntington, IN: Our Sunday Visitor, 2006.

Kaczor, Christopher. *Thomas Aquinas on Faith, Hope, and Love: Edited and Explained for Everyone*. Ave Maria, FL: Sapientia, 2008.

Kaczor, Christopher, and Thomas Sherman. *Thomas Aquinas on the Cardinal Virtues: Edited and Explained for Everyone*. Ave Maria, FL: Sapientia, 2009.

Keenan, James F. *Virtues for Ordinary Christians*. Kansas City, MO: Sheed & Ward, 1996.

Kreeft, Peter. *Back to Virtue: Traditional Moral Wisdom for Modern Moral Confusion*. San Francisco: Ignatius, 1992.

Mattison, William C., III. *Introducing Moral Theology: True Happiness and the Virtues*. Grand Rapids: Brazos, 2008.

Pieper, Josef. *A Brief Reader on the Virtues of the Human Heart*. Translated by Paul C. Duggan. San Francisco: Ignatius, 1991.

———. *The Four Cardinal Virtues: Prudence, Justice, Fortitude, Temperance*. Notre Dame: University of Notre Dame Press, 1966.

Pope, Stephen J., ed. *The Ethics of Aquinas*. Washington, DC: Georgetown University Press, 2002.

INDEX

Made in the USA
Middletown, DE
01 August 2021